T0316577

Cambridge Elements

Elements in Ethics
edited by
Ben Eggleston
University of Kansas
Dale E. Miller
Old Dominion University, Virginia

HAPPINESS
AND WELL-BEING

Chris Heathwood
University of Colorado Boulder

CAMBRIDGE
UNIVERSITY PRESS

CAMBRIDGE
UNIVERSITY PRESS

University Printing House, Cambridge CB2 8BS, United Kingdom

One Liberty Plaza, 20th Floor, New York, NY 10006, USA

477 Williamstown Road, Port Melbourne, VIC 3207, Australia

314–321, 3rd Floor, Plot 3, Splendor Forum, Jasola District Centre,
New Delhi – 110025, India

103 Penang Road, #05–06/07, Visioncrest Commercial, Singapore 238467

Cambridge University Press is part of the University of Cambridge.

It furthers the University's mission by disseminating knowledge in the pursuit of
education, learning, and research at the highest international levels of excellence.

www.cambridge.org
Information on this title:www.cambridge.org/9781108706407
DOI: 10.1017/9781108580830

First published 2021

A catalogue record for this publication is available from the British Library.

ISBN 978-1-108-70640-7 Paperback
ISSN 2516-4031 (online)
ISSN 2516-4023 (print)

Happiness and Well-Being

Elements in Ethics

DOI: 10.1017/9781108580830
First published online: October 2021

Chris Heathwood
University of Colorado Boulder

Author for correspondence: Chris Heathwood, heathwood@colorado.edu

Abstract: This Element provides an opinionated introduction to the debate in moral philosophy over identifying the basic elements of well-being and to the related debate over the nature of happiness. The question of the nature of happiness is simply the question of what happiness *is* (as opposed to what causes it or how to get it), and the central philosophical question about well-being is the question of what things are in themselves of ultimate benefit or harm to a person, or directly make them better or worse off.

Keywords: happiness, welfare, quality of life, pleasure, life satisfaction

ISBNs: 9781108706407 (PB), 9781108580830 (OC)
ISSNs: 2516-4031 (online), 2516-4023 (print)

Contents

1 The Topics of Well-Being and Happiness

I write these words from my home in Boulder, Colorado, which a recent *National Geographic*/Gallup study named "the happiest place in the United States." It was claimed furthermore that Boulder "produces the highest level of well-being for its residents" and that people in Boulder "live better lives" than do people in any other US city surveyed (Buettner 2017).

How do studies like this one purport to measure happiness, and how can we be sure that what they are measuring is the genuine article? Being confident of this requires having some idea of what happiness is. And even if we know what happiness is and how to measure it, are we allowed to infer conclusions about well-being or about the value of a life from premises about happiness?

This Element is about these more fundamental, more philosophical questions that lie behind happiness studies of this sort. Such studies often simply assume certain answers to these questions. In this Element, we'll examine these assumptions. We'll be exploring, centrally, these two questions: 1) What is happiness? and 2) What is ultimately in a person's interests? *Happiness and Well-Being.*

Any answers to these ancient, awesome questions are going to be controversial, and we will get to these controversies. But there is disagreement even in how to understand the questions themselves. This first section clarifies our questions, focusing mainly on the question about well-being, and touches on how we might try to answer them.

1.1 Ways a Life Can Be Good

Start with this question: *What makes a life a good life?* It is hard to imagine a more important question. The title of this Element, however, mentions not "a good life" but "well-being." Is that difference important?

Yes. When we talk about well-being, I think we are talking about a phenomenon narrower than that of the goodness of a life. I take the philosophical question of well-being to be the question of what things are of ultimate *benefit or harm* to us and other beings capable of being benefitted and harmed. It may help to put the question in other ways as well; indeed, I think that clarifying the question in ordinary language is our best means of getting at it. Some different ways of asking the philosophical question of well-being:

What is of *ultimate benefit or harm* to beings capable of being benefitted and harmed?
What *directly* makes a being *better or worse off*?
What things are good or bad in themselves *for* some being?
What is in or against a being's *self-interest*?

Two other terms for well-being are *welfare* and *prudential value*.

The concept of a good life is a broader concept. Having positive well-being is one way in which a life can be good, but not the only way. Understanding some of these other ways serves to distinguish well-being not only from a good life more generally but from these other more specific ways in which a life can be good.

1.1.1 Moral Goodness

One of these more specific ways is *moral goodness*. How a life rates morally can diverge from how it rates self-interestedly. To see this, let's consider an example in some detail. For the purposes of this illustration, let's assume that there are strong moral reasons against buying and consuming meat from factory farms. And let's assume that this is owing to the great suffering factory farming visits on sentient creatures, to its significant environmental costs, and to the risks it creates of spreading infectious diseases among humans. Now suppose that Korva, a college student, loves eating meat. She never feels fully satiated after a meatless meal. Eating meat is, moreover, a deeply engrained part of her social and cultural life. Unfortunately, non-factory-raised meat is not available where Korva lives.

Korva's philosophy class is spending two weeks on the ethics of eating meat. Although she has been vaguely aware of some moral arguments on the topic, studying the matter in a serious way increases her appreciation of the strong moral reasons she has to stop eating meat. At the end of this unit in her course, she feels greater motivation to become a vegetarian than ever before. She feels herself at a crossroads: If she is ever going to quit this practice, one that she has come to think of as indefensible, now is the time. Depending on what Korva decides to do today, one of these two futures will come about:

M: Korva decides that she just cannot make what she sees as such a disruptive lifestyle change. She remains a meat eater for the rest of her life. She has occasional thoughts that her diet is morally problematic, but they are rare, in part because no one around her takes seriously the idea that there is anything wrong with eating meat. More often when Korva thinks of vegetarianism, she is amazed that she was at one point seriously considering becoming a vegetarian. On the whole, Korva feels good about herself and the way she leads her life.

V: In what she takes to be a moment of moral clarity and courage, Korva resolves to give up meat once and for all. In part to hold herself accountable, she announces her new commitment to her friends and family. She finds her new lifestyle difficult. She never enjoys her meals as much as she used to, and secretly envies her friends for their more carefree, indulgent lifestyles. She even finds that her vegetarianism is something of a barrier between herself and her friends and family. They never tire of poking fun at her about it. She socializes less with them and feels less connected to them when she does. Korva also lacks the information she needs to ensure that her new diet is healthful, and her health suffers as a result. But she remains convinced that this is the virtuous path and the one required by morality.

I have laid this out in some detail because I want us to be able to make relatively confident moral and prudential evaluations of Korva's two possible futures. Our questions are these. In which life, M or V, is Korva herself better off? And in which life, M or V, is she leading a morally better life? Recall that we simply *stipulated* for the purposes of this example that there are, in fact, very strong moral reasons not to buy and eat meat from factory farms.

I assume you agree that life M is prudentially better for Korva than is life V, while life V is morally better. We can leave aside the question of which life is the better life *overall*, or the life that, all things considered, Korva should choose to lead. The fact that the possible life that is prudentially better for Korva is not the one that is morally better helps us to see the difference between prudential and moral goodness.

1.1.2 Other Scales of Evaluation

Although morality and prudence are the evaluative domains most discussed by philosophers, we make other important evaluations of our lives. For example, we think about how *meaningful* they are. As with moral goodness, it appears that how meaningful a life is can vary independently from how beneficial it is to the person living it. Perhaps the case of Korva shows this, since it may be that supporting a morally good cause at the expense of your own self-interest makes your life more meaningful.

A fourth respect in which a life can be a good one, or worth choosing – in addition to its having prudential value, moral value, and meaning – is by its manifesting *excellence*. A life manifests excellence to the extent that the person living it excels at certain worthwhile activities. The possibilities here are endless: chess, boxing, jazz trombone, table tennis, Scrabble, Hatha yoga, oil painting, StarCraft, hip-hop dance. This good-making feature of a life can also come apart from well-being. It is a truism that learning to master a difficult activity can require sacrifice. The sacrifice is to one's well-being.

That a life would benefit the person living it is surely a reason for that person to choose that life. Not a decisive reason, but a reason nonetheless. The same is true for the life's involving moral virtue, meaning, and excellence. In other words, each of these four domains of evaluation is a way that a life can be good. This shows that the notion of a good life is a wider notion than that of a life that is good *for* the person living it ("good *for*" signals well-being). Thus, if the author of the *National Geographic* article slides from the idea that a certain group of people tends to be well-off to the idea that they are getting good lives, that is a little hasty. If these people tend to have, say, morally corrupt and meaningless lives, their being well-off may not be enough to make their lives good overall.

1.2 More on the Philosophical Question of Well-Being

Also incautious would be a slide from the idea that a person is very happy to the idea that they are very well-off. The theory that the single fundamental ingredient of human well-being is happiness is just one possible answer to the philosophical question about well-being.

A further clarification about that question: When we ask it, we are not asking about the *causes* of well-being; we are asking what things *in themselves* make a person better off. If someone were asked simply to list "some things off the top of your head that benefit a person," maybe their list would include the following: Winning the lottery, visiting the dentist twice a year, getting eight hours of sleep each night, spending time in nature, and warm hugs. For many of us, these are indeed good things. But are they good things to get *in themselves*, or is their value instead derivative – inherited from other things that it is good to get and that these things help us to get?

One method for deciding this is to imagine a situation in which some person gets the thing in question but fails to get any of its usual effects or accompaniments. Then we ask ourselves whether it still seems like a good thing for them that they got it. So, imagine that someone *wins the lottery*, but that every last penny of their winnings is quickly lost in a harebrained investment scheme. Or we can ask whether a person who has no teeth would still benefit from visiting the dentist every six months. Or we can imagine someone having a hug forced on them when all they want is to be left alone. In these cases, the thing in question (the winning of the lottery, the dental visits, the hug) seems to be of no benefit at all. This suggests that it isn't *that very thing* that is the benefit but some other thing that usually accompanies it.

We are here homing in on the distinction between a thing's being good for someone *derivatively*, due to its being connected in a certain way to something of more fundamental value for them, and a thing's being good for someone in this more basic way. I will usually refer to this as the distinction between a thing's being *derivatively good* for someone and a thing's being *basically good* for them. Philosophers also speak of a thing's being *instrumentally good* for someone as opposed to *intrinsically good* for them.

The philosophical question of well-being concerns what is *basically* good for us. That is why the formulations above mentioned *ultimate* benefit and harm and spoke of what *directly* makes us better or worse off. These are simply different ways of conveying the all-important notion of basic value. Some of our formulations also spoke of what things are good or bad *in themselves* for us, which invokes this same idea.

1.2.1 Why Philosophers of Well-Being Focus on Basic *Prudential Value*

The question of what is basically good for subjects of welfare is, by definition, more fundamental than the question of what is derivatively good for them. Derivative value is definable in terms of basic value, roughly as follows: A thing is derivatively good for a person if and only if it is appropriately related to something that is basically good for them. The most obvious such relation is *causation*: If x causes y and y is basically good for a certain subject – as when taking a sip of coffee causes a pleasant taste experience – then x will thereby be derivatively good for that subject. Other such relations are *prevention* (it's good to get anesthetic because it prevents pain), *signification* (it's good if your medical test comes back negative because that is a sign of good health), and *parthood* (if an evening contains a bunch of good moments, that can make the evening itself good, albeit derivatively so). Because philosophers tend to be interested in the most fundamental aspects of whatever they are studying, it is no surprise that philosophers of welfare are most interested in basic welfare value.

Another reason it makes sense for philosophers to focus on basic rather than derivative value is epistemological. Questions of basic value can arguably be answered *a priori*, whereas questions of derivative value – being in part questions about what causes what, what prevents what, and so on – are partly *empirical* and thus ill-suited to investigation from the philosopher's armchair. The empirical/a priori distinction is an epistemological distinction, or a distinction having to do with how we come to know about reality. To know something empirically is to know it using your senses, including introspection (or to know it by reasoning exclusively from facts so discovered). Empirical knowledge is observational knowledge. To know something a priori is to know it absent any empirical investigation or evidence.

To illustrate, I know empirically *that there are limes in my refrigerator* (by using my eyes) and *that I am craving a margarita* (by introspecting). Two other things that I know are *that all triangles have three sides* and *that nothing can be red and green all over at the same time*; but I don't have to use my senses to verify these things. Simply understanding what these claims are saying puts us in a position to know them without the benefit of any empirical evidence. Thus we know them a priori.

A priori knowledge was defined negatively, simply as knowledge that is not empirical; so we know what its source is not (empirical observation). Can we say what its source is? One answer, and an answer that fits well with common practice in ethics, is *rational intuition*. Rational intuitions are states of mind in which we can "just see" that some claim is true, or in which we feel compelled to believe the claim, simply on the basis of what the claim is saying. We have rational intuitions about a wide variety of topics, including ethics. For example, virtually everyone has the intuition that *it's wrong to set a cat on fire for fun* and that *pain is bad in itself.*

Those intuitions are about general claims. When doing ethics, we frequently consider particular cases as well. But they are cases whose empirical aspects are stipulated, and so when we make value judgments about them, such judgments are a priori. Such cases are often used to help us discover general principles, and to test them. This is the method that will be on display throughout this Element, when it comes to discovering both the elements of well-being and the nature of happiness.

Curiously, although the partly empirical question of the causes of well-being is parasitic on the a priori matter of what the basic prudential goods are, the causal question seems easier to answer. Steven Pinker's recent book *Enlightenment Now* contains a chapter on each of about a dozen things that he assumes without argument are conducive to human well-being; they include longevity, health, sustenance, wealth, peace, safety, equal rights, knowledge, and happiness (Pinker 2018). And there is indeed no serious dispute over whether these are important promoters of human well-being. But things are different when it comes to the underlying question of why. The question of what the basic elements of well-being are, which would explain and justify Pinker's list, is evidently much harder to answer, as shown by the widespread disagreement over this question among philosophers of well-being. As a work about the philosophy rather than the science or economics of well-being, this Element's focus will be on the harder, more fundamental, philosophical question.

1.3 The Question of the Nature of Happiness

Another of this Element's goals is to investigate the nature of happiness. Here we are, wanting to know not *what makes* us happy, but *what it is to be* happy.

This first pass at our question is only as clear as the terms in it. But the term "happy" is ambiguous. Thus we don't yet know what thing it is whose nature we seek to understand. What are the various phenomena that travel under the label "happiness"?

Unfortunately, there is disagreement about even this. That is, in addition to metaphysical disagreement about the nature of whatever phenomena the word "happiness" might stand for, there is linguistic disagreement over just what phenomena the term signifies in the first place. This linguistic disagreement notwithstanding, in Section 3 we will distinguish three central notions of happiness, which will be our focus.

1.3.1 Happiness and Well-Being

So how do these two phenomena, happiness and well-being, which supply the title of our Element, relate to one another? This is a matter of controversy, a controversy we'll wade into, but a way in which they might be related is that happiness is one of the basic prudential goods. That is, it makes people better off, all else equal, when they are happier. Indeed, this might sound too obvious to be worth stating. A stronger and much more controversial claim about the relation between happiness and well-being has it that happiness is the *sole* prudential good, so that a person is well-off just to the extent that they are happy.

But we are here encroaching on the topic of some of the sections to come: possible answers to the philosophical question of well-being. Our exploration of what things are of ultimate benefit and harm to a person will begin with an examination of one of the most central questions about well-being: is it *objective* or *subjective*?

2 Objectivism and Subjectivism about Well-Being

2.1 A Preliminary List

The philosophical question of well-being asks what things in themselves make a subject better or worse off. Now that we better understand the question, how do we go about answering it? It is reasonable to begin with our initial intuitions, or how things first seem to us. The philosopher William Frankena began this way and came up with an impressively long preliminary list:

> Life, consciousness, and activity
> Health and strength
> Pleasures and satisfactions of all or certain kinds
> Happiness, beatitude, contentment, etc.

Truth
Knowledge and true opinion of various kinds, understanding, wisdom
Beauty, harmony, proportion in objects contemplated
Aesthetic experience
Morally good dispositions or virtues
Mutual affection, love, friendship, cooperation
Just distribution of goods and evils
Harmony and proportion in one's own life
Power and experiences of achievement
Self-expression
Freedom
Peace, security
Adventure and novelty
Good reputation, honor, esteem, etc. (Frankena 1973: 87–8)

At a quick first pass, nothing seems terribly out of place. Each of these seems like a pretty good thing to have in your life. All of these words at least have "positive valence." But a little reflection reveals that the list can be refined and reduced.

Some entries seem redundant. Take "Truth," for instance. What is it to have truth in your life? Presumably this: To know, or at least to believe, some true things. But, as Frankena recognizes (1973: 89), that is covered by the next item on the list, "Knowledge and true opinion of various kinds." So "Truth" should be deleted.

Other items have the following feature: some but not all instances of them seem good. This is a problem because the appearance of the item on the list is presumably meant to imply that every instance of the item would be good to have. So take "activity." Some activities, such as playing a sport you love or summitting a beautiful mountain, seem good, but other activities, such as trudging barefoot through the snow or riding a vomit-inducing carnival ride, seem positively bad. Perhaps, then, we'd want to modify "activity" to something more specific. One option is "enjoyable activity," although then the item might be rendered redundant, since "Pleasure" appears already.

Those were some of the lower-hanging fruit, but other items should also be removed. In my view, one of them is "Health." It is obvious that health is almost always a good thing to have, but that may just be because health is of merely derivative value. How do we decide whether the obvious goodness of health is wholly derivative or at least partly basic?

2.2 A Test for Basic Goodness

We can use the following test. We imagine a pair of cases that differ in a minimal way – "minimal pairs." They differ just with respect to the putative basic good in question and are otherwise as alike as possible. Then we consult our intuitions about the cases. Does it seem to us that the case with the putative good added contains more well-being than its minimal pair? If the answer is "yes," then this is evidence that the good in question is a basic good. That's because, if the cases are minimal pairs, then they won't differ with respect to the effects or other accompaniments of the putative good. So the difference in value that we intuit must lie in the presence of the putative good itself. If, by contrast, it does *not* seem that the case featuring the putative good is any better than the variant that lacks it, this is evidence that the putative good is not a genuine basic good after all.

Here is a minimal pair that we can use to test whether health is of intrinsic welfare value:

Coma: Giles is in a terrible accident and falls into a coma. Although his brain is damaged, the rest of his body is a specimen of perfect health. Two days later, Giles dies.

Coma Minus: Giles is in a terrible accident and falls into a coma. Although his brain is damaged, the rest of his body is a specimen of near-perfect health. His only health defect is a minor renal contusion, caused by the accident, which makes one of Giles's kidneys function slightly less well. Two days later, Giles dies.

The only difference between this minimal pair is that one of Giles's kidneys is slightly impaired in Coma Minus, making him in slightly worse physical health. All else is equal, including all of Giles's experiences and the time and manner of Giles's death. So, consider the period of time during which Giles is lying in a coma in the hospital bed. *During this period, is Giles better off in Coma than he is in Coma Minus?*

It seems to me that the answer is "no." Although Giles is indeed healthier in Coma than he is in Coma Minus, this superior health does him no good. I don't think this is a hard case either; I feel quite confident that Giles is no better off in Coma than in Coma Minus. Because the view that health is among the basic welfare goods implies otherwise, we should remove "Health" from the list.

Similar reasoning shows that "Life" is of no basic welfare value either. Consider a new case, *Coma Plus*, exactly like Coma except that, in Coma Plus, Giles lives for an additional day. Since, I hope you agree, his getting to be alive (but still comatose) for this additional day is no benefit to him, "Life" should also be removed from our list.

The same goes for "Consciousness," it seems to me. Consider *Coma Plus Flicker*. It is exactly like Coma except that one evening in which Giles is lying in a coma, he experiences a dim flicker of consciousness for a few moments. Some random neuronal activity in his brain causes him to experience a low-volume auditory hum for a few moments. The sound sensation does not cause him to have any thoughts: It doesn't startle him; it doesn't make him wonder where he is or make him have hopeful thoughts that he might regain full consciousness; it doesn't make him afraid. He is no longer capable of having any such thoughts or emotions. Nor is the auditory hum pleasant or unpleasant in any way. It is simply an isolated flicker of conscious experience. It seems to me that this brief, dim, conscious experience doesn't make Giles's life better in any way. But the hypothesis that consciousness itself is a basic welfare good implies otherwise. Thus, "Consciousness" should also be removed from our list.

2.2.1 Not Everything Fails the Test

But not every item on Frankena's list fails this test. That would be bad news for the test; it would call its validity into question. One item that seems to pass the test is "Happiness." Consider *Coma Plus Happiness*. It is just like Coma except that Giles wakes up for a few brief moments, sees that he is alive, sees his family in the room, and is happy to see them. We can suppose that this happiness is short-lived. Giles falls back into the coma and succumbs to his condition shortly thereafter.

Was Giles's experiencing this brief moment of happiness a good thing for him? Although I don't have a highly confident reaction to this unusual case, I am inclined to think that the answer is "yes." Granted it wasn't *highly valuable*, brief as it was. But I have experienced brief moments of happiness as Giles did, and they were good experiences for me.

I believe that several other items on Frankena's list – in particular, "Pleasures and satisfactions" (at least "of certain kinds"), "beatitude," "contentment," "Knowledge" (and related phenomena), and "Aesthetic experience" – pass this test in the same sort of way.

I'm not sure if this sort of test can be used to evaluate every item on Frankena's list, however. For example, it may not be easy to evaluate "Mutual affection, love, friendship, cooperation" and "Harmony and proportion in one's own life" using a case that differs only minimally from Coma.

2.3 The *Euthyphro* Question about Well-Being and Another Test

But we can scrutinize these putative goods in other ways. Take "friendship." I am very glad to have friends in my life and it certainly seems to me that they make my life better. And it is a common and plausible thought that we value our friends and our friendships for their own sake rather than for other goods that they might bring us. The same might be true for some of the other goods on the list, such as "Freedom," "Adventure," and "Good reputation." Each of these is a thing that many of us want in our lives and at least in part for its own sake.

But this brings us to a question of central importance in the philosophy of well-being:

Do we want and enjoy these things in our lives because it is good to have them, or is it good to have them because we want and enjoy them?

This may remind some readers of a famous question asked by Socrates in Plato's *Euthyphro* (c. 380 BCE). Socrates's question was about piety and its relation to what the gods care about. But it is common nowadays, and deeply interesting, to consider the question as if it were about morality. Thus one variant of Socrates's question is this: "Is an action wrong because God forbids it, or does God forbid it because it is wrong?" Another variant is non-theistic: "Is an action wrong because we disapprove of it, or do we disapprove of it because it is wrong?"

Ignoring certain quibbles and complexities, *objectivists about morality* say that we disapprove of wrong acts because they are wrong, these acts being wrong independently of what anyone thinks or feels about them. *Subjectivists about morality* maintain that wrong actions are wrong because we disapprove of them. On this view, moral facts are in some way constructed out of our subjective reactions to the world rather than being themselves a part of the fabric of objective reality.

The same categories can be found on the topic of well-being. *Objectivists about well-being* hold that we want and enjoy things such as friendship, knowledge, freedom, and good repute because it is good for us to have these things independently of whether we want or enjoy them, our positive attitudes toward them being fitting reactions to their objective prudential value. *Subjectivists about well-being* hold that nothing is good for people in this attitude-independent way; things are good for us only when we take up positive attitudes toward them, and only on account of these attitudes. Philosophers sometimes use the term "pro-attitude" to mean the same thing as "positive attitude," and we'll sometimes use that term as well.[1]

Returning to morality, consider the fact that it is wrong to light a cat on fire for fun. To me, the wrongness here seems objective. We don't think of the wrongness of this act as contingent on our disapproving it. If the sociopaths who revel

---

[1] One quibble worth mentioning is that it is actually no part of objectivism about well-being to offer a psychological explanation of why we want and enjoy the things we want and enjoy (nor is it any part of objectivism about morality to offer a psychological explanation of why people disapprove of what they disapprove of). We'll offer a more proper characterization of objectivism about well-being below.

in this activity manage to convince every last one of us that setting cats on fire is just innocent fun, its moral heinousness would not thereby be erased; we would just have become blind to it.

What about well-being? Consider the fact that friendship is good, that it makes our lives better. Is the presence of friendship in a person's life a good thing for that person only because the person wants it, likes it, enjoys it, or cares to have it in their life? Or would friendship be a good thing for the person to have even if they lacked any desire for it, never enjoyed it, had no interest in it, and it got them nothing else that they wanted, liked, enjoyed, or cared to have?

In trying to answer this crucial question, it can help to consider concrete cases. So consider Ira:

> Ira is a happy, high-functioning autistic man. He knows that friends are something that people are supposed to have, but he gets no pleasure from being around other people. He doesn't enjoy sharing his thoughts and feelings, or his life more generally, with anyone. He would rather do the things he likes to do – hiking, following baseball, listening to classical music – alone. He did dutifully maintain friendships in his twenties because he had been told to seek and maintain them. But they never ceased feeling like things he was obligated to be involved with rather than things he wanted to be involved with. Ira himself would say that all his time with his friends felt detached. Being self-sufficient and strongly averse to asking anyone for anything, having friends never got him anything else he wanted either. Luckily, he never needed friends for anything either. He always managed to take care of his business himself. By the end of his twenties, Ira came to believe that his friendships were doing nothing for him and let himself drift apart from all of his friends. Once he did, he wondered why he hadn't done it sooner.

What is your reaction to Ira's case? Did his having friends make him any better off? For me, the verdict is clear: Ira's friendships were of no benefit to him.

This is exactly unlike the case of morality. The wrongness of setting light to a cat does not seem at all beholden to our thinking it wrong or disapproving of it. When we imagine the odd scenario in which no one disapproves of this act, we still think that the act is wrong in that scenario (although no one in the scenario realizes it). Not so in the case of well-being. When I imagine the odd scenario above in which some person has no positive attitudes toward his friendships, what they involve, and what else they get him, I no longer think that his friendships are of any benefit to him.

This shows, in my view, that "Friendship" does not belong on our list of basic goods. If friendship were a basic good, then we should have the reaction that Ira's life was made better by his friendships. Instead, it seems that when friendship is good for some subject that is only because it bears some connection to positive attitudes on the part of the subject.

We can run a similar test for other goods. Take "knowledge." Imagine a student, Doualy, who reads Frankena's list, knows that Frankena is an expert in moral philosophy, and, in an attempt to get a better life, pursues knowledge for its own sake. She dutifully takes a course in medieval Japanese history and acquires a working knowledge of the Kamakura and Muromachi periods. Doualy finds, however, that her new expertise does nothing for her. She has no interest in what she has learned, is not glad she learned it, and never will be. It also happens to be of no use to her: it never helps her understand anything that she does care to know, and she never impresses anyone with it at dinner parties. Still, she did gain and continues to retain this new knowledge.

Is Doualy benefitted by the presence of the extra supply of knowledge? As with the case of Ira, it seems that the answer is "no." But then "Knowledge" does not belong on our list of basic goods either. *Knowledge that we are glad to have* plausibly benefits us, but knowledge that forever leaves us cold, and doesn't enable us to get any other goods or avoid any bads, has no positive effect on our well-being.

With similar sorts of thought experiment, I think we can show the same thing about a bunch of other items on Frankena's list: cooperation, harmony and proportion in one's own life, power, experiences of achievement, self-expression, freedom, peace, security, adventure, novelty, good reputation, and esteem.

2.3.1 Not Everything Fails This Test Either

But not all of the items on Frankena's list fail this "but-what-if-the-putative-good-leaves-you-cold?" test. That's because some putative goods, by their nature, *can't* leave you cold. Take "Pleasures and satisfactions of all or certain kinds." Imagine Lakshmi, who spends the week refinishing the floors in her house and is very pleased with the results. The state of her floors definitely does not leave her cold; she loves how they look and feel. And the same would be true in any possible case of *being pleased with something*. If you are pleased with something, you thereby have a positive attitude toward it; being pleased *just is* a positive attitude. This was not the case with friendship and knowledge – you can have those while lacking pro-attitudes toward them or toward anything else[2] – and that is why they don't always seem beneficial to us.

---

[2] It is worth reflecting on whether it really is true that you can have friendship while lacking positive attitudes. Might it be that to count as being in a friendship, you need to have certain positive attitudes toward it or toward your friend? See Fletcher 2013.

All of this points toward an answer to the Euthyphro question about well-being: it's not that we want and enjoy the things in our lives because it is independently good to have them; rather, it is good to have them because we want and enjoy them. In a nutshell, subjectivism about well-being seems more plausible than objectivism. If prudential value is indeed subjective, this may be related to the fact that prudential value is itself subject-*relative*: well-being is always goodness *for* some subject (Sumner 1996: ch. 2).

There are two problems of detail here that we need to iron out. We began with the Euthyphro question about well-being. We ran some tests suggesting that the subjectivist answer is the right one. We designed the cases in these tests so that the subject had no positive attitudes toward the putative good in question. Then I claimed that some goods, such as being pleased with something, are guaranteed to pass the test because they *just are* positive attitudes. But here is the first problem of detail. The lesson we were supposed to have learned from the cases is roughly that *something can directly benefit you only if you have a positive attitude toward it*. But Lakshmi may have no positive attitude toward *the fact that she is pleased* with her floors; her positive attitude is simply with the floors themselves. So the putative good of "being pleased with something," while it may pass the spirit of the lesson we learned, does not pass the letter of it – at least as I worded the lesson above.

The solution is to broaden the letter of the lesson we have learned. The lesson, thus worded, is that a thing is basically good for some subject only if *either* it is a thing that the subject has a pro-attitude toward *or* it involves the subject's having a pro-attitude toward something. So, in the case of Lakshmi, if we want to say that the basically good thing for her is *her having beautiful floors*, that claim conforms to the lesson we have learned. But if we want instead to say that the basically good thing for her is *her being pleased with her beautiful floors*, this claim also conforms to the lesson we have learned, under the new, broader formulation. However we prefer to describe the basic good on the scene, it is a basic good that conforms to our lesson.

That was the first problem of detail. The second problem of detail has to do with the fact that while for some positive attitudes (like being pleased with something) the mere having of the attitude is plausibly regarded as sufficient for benefit, for other positive attitudes, the mere having of them is obviously not sufficient for benefit. We should want our statement of the lesson we have learned from the cases above to be sensitive to this. The most familiar pro-attitude the mere having of which is obviously insufficient for benefit is *desire*. Merely wanting something to be the case is obviously not enough to be benefitted. One thing that is different between attitudes like desiring that something be the case and attitudes like being pleased that something is the case is that only the latter sorts of attitude entail that the subject having the attitude *believes that the object of the attitude obtains or is true.* For some such attitudes, the having of the attitude may even entail that the object of the attitude *really does obtain or really is true.*

Taking our cue from this, let's introduce a special notion of what it is for an attitude to be "satisfied." When we say that an attitude is satisfied, we will mean that the object of the attitude either obtains or is believed by the subject having the attitude to obtain. Thus, if I want it to be snowing in the mountains right now, this want is satisfied, in our special sense, if either I believe that it is snowing in the mountains or it really is snowing in the mountains. Note that if I am *pleased* that it is snowing in the mountains – or, more generally, am pleased about whatever – then this pro-attitude is automatically satisfied in our sense; that's because you can be pleased that something is the case only if you believe that it is the case.

With this account of attitude satisfaction in place, we can now more accurately state the lesson that we learned from the cases above (of Ira, Doualy, and Lakshmi). It is that a thing is basically good for some subject only if either it is a thing that the subject has a *satisfied* pro-attitude toward *or* it involves the subject's having a *satisfied* pro-attitude toward something.

2.3.2 The Resonance Constraint on Well-Being

It is worth stating this lesson more explicitly still. We have essentially been working up to a certain important doctrine about well-being, sometimes referred to as the

Resonance Constraint: a thing, x, is basically good for some subject, S, only if *either* S has a satisfied positive attitude toward x *or* x itself involves S's having a satisfied positive attitude toward something.

The thought experiments conducted above give us reason to think that the resonance constraint is true. And if it is true, this gives us reason to think that subjectivism rather than objectivism about well-being is true.

To illustrate the resonance constraint further, another item on Frankena's list that satisfies it is "Happiness." Suppose that Shay gets a raise and is happy about that. The claim that her being happy about the raise is a good thing for her conforms to the resonance constraint because her being happy about the raise just is her having a satisfied pro-attitude toward something (happiness is certainly a positive attitude, and it is one of those attitudes that are automatically satisfied, because being happy that something is the case requires believing that it is the case). On an intuitive level, this is a state that is not leaving Shay cold. You are not being left cold in some situation if you are happy about something in that situation.

2.4 Subjectivism vs. Objectivism about Well-Being

Earlier we said that subjectivism about well-being is roughly the view that whenever something is basically good for us, this is in virtue of the positive attitudes we take up toward it. Let's now state the doctrine more officially.

2.4.1 Subjectivism about Well-Being

Our formulation will make use of the two ways that a theory of well-being can be "pro-attitude involving," which we became acquainted with in our presentation of the resonance constraint, and it will also make use of our special notion of pro-attitude satisfaction:

Subjectivism about well-being: Something is basically good for a subject if and only if either the subject has a certain satisfied pro-attitude toward it, or it involves the having of a certain satisfied pro-attitude of theirs toward something.

The "something" there at the end should be interpreted in such a way that there are no restrictions on what the subject might have positive attitudes toward; she can be into whatever she likes. (For simplicity of presentation, I did not include merely hypothetical attitudes in the definition, which are needed to cover so-called idealized theories, which we'll discuss later; I have also left implicit the corresponding doctrine about badness for a subject.)

To illustrate this definition, consider a theory of well-being according to which the states that are basically good for a subject are states in which the subject is happy about something. This *happiness theory* counts as a subjective theory because, on it, the things that are basically good for subjects of welfare are states in which the subject is having a satisfied positive attitude (happiness) toward something. Or consider a theory on which a thing is basically good for a person if and only if it is something the person wants for its own sake. This *desire-satisfaction theory* counts as subjective because, on it, the things that are basically good for subjects of welfare are things the subject has a satisfied positive attitude (desire) toward. We will examine these and other species of subjectivism in Section 4.

2.4.2 Objectivism about Well-Being

Despite its appeal, subjectivism faces important objections. These motivate some to endorse its archrival, objectivism. According to

Objectivism about well-being: At least one thing that is basically good for subjects of welfare is not "pro-attitude-involving," in the sense of necessarily being either the object of a satisfied positive attitude on the subject's part or involving the subject's having a satisfied positive attitude toward something.

When one first attempts to answer the philosophical question of well-being, one might naturally begin, as Frankena essentially did, by constructing a version of what is known as the *objective-list theory*, one of the two main varieties of objectivism about well-being. The objective-list theory combines objectivism about well-being with *pluralism*, the view that there is more than one basic welfare good.

Frankena's preliminary list above would constitute the core of an objective-list theory, albeit one with an unusually long list. Philosopher Derek Parfit mentions "the development of one's abilities, knowledge, and the awareness of true beauty" as plausible objective welfare goods (Parfit 1984: 3). The objective list of philosopher James Griffin comprises, roughly, accomplishment, autonomy, understanding, enjoyment, and deep personal relations (Griffin 1986: 67–8). Philosopher Martha Nussbaum's list is longer, and includes life, health, bodily integrity, emotional attachment, practical reason, affiliation, play, and more (Nussbaum 2000: 77–80). Psychologist Martin Seligman has an acronym for his list: PERMA stands for positive emotion, engagement (the feeling of being lost in a task), relationships, meaning, and accomplishment (Seligman 2011).

These lists may strike some as parochial or bourgeois. Genghis Khan is reported to have offered a less conventional list: "[t]o crush your enemies, to see them fall at your feet, to take their horses and goods, and to hear the lamentation of their women. That is best" (Lamb 1927: 107; lightly edited for readability). But some non-Western intellectual traditions have produced lists similar to those above; for example, on one interpretation, Buddhism puts forth life, knowledge, and friendship as the three basic prudential goods (Keown 1995: 42–3).

The other leading version of objectivism about well-being is *perfectionism*, the main monistic form of objectivism ("monistic" in that it puts forth just one basic good, in contrast to pluralistic theories, which put forth more than one). Perfectionism involves the intuitive idea that in order to know how well-off some subject of welfare is, we first have to know that subject's *nature*. On perfectionism, subjects of welfare are better off just when their natures have been more fully developed, realized, or exercised. Thus, for perfectionists to offer a determinate theory of human welfare, they must have an account of human nature. Many perfectionists hold that rationality is a part of human nature and thus that people are better off, all else equal, the more developed their rational capacities are and/or the more they exercise them. Some perfectionists hold something similar for moral and physical capacities. The most important perfectionist in the history of Western philosophy is the ancient Greek philosopher Aristotle. Other historically important perfectionists include the Confucian philosopher Mencius, the medieval Catholic philosopher Thomas Aquinas, and the nineteenth-century German philosophers Karl Marx and Friedrich Nietzsche (see Fletcher 2016 for more on perfectionism and its history).

2.4.3 The Debate Between Subjectivists and Objectivists

In my view, the main reason to think that subjectivism rather than objectivism is the right approach to well-being is that subjectivism conforms to the resonance constraint – a compelling and widely shared intuition about well-being – while objectivism does not. Subjectivism also accommodates our intuitions about the particular cases that support the resonance constraint. There are other reasons to be a subjectivist having to do with certain somewhat abstruse doctrines in moral philosophy. We'll skip these and move on to considerations that favor objectivism, alongside some subjectivist rebuttals. We'll conclude this subsection with some challenges to objectivism, alongside objectivist rebuttals.

Challenges to Subjectivist Views

Immoral Desires, Stupid Desires. It seems possible to want or like the wrong things. This is clearest with malicious, sadistic, or otherwise immoral desires. According to someone who knew him, serial killer and rapist Ted Bundy was "a sadistic sociopath who took pleasure from another human's pain" as well as from "the control he had over his victims, to the point of death, and even after" (Rule 2009: xiv). It is impossible to be certain just how Bundy felt about his life and his behavior, but let's suppose, for the sake of argument, that he wholeheartedly endorsed his lifestyle and never felt an iota of compunction about it. Bundy was eventually caught and executed for his crimes, but let's consider the life he led up until the time he was caught. Was that a good life?

Now, our question is not: "Was that a *morally* good life?" The answer to that question is obvious. Our question is: "Was it good *for Bundy*?" On the assumptions that he "loved every minute" of his life, that he endorsed it, and valued it, and believed it to be good, and, furthermore, would have endorsed it after careful reflection and after clearing up any misconceptions he had about it, it follows that pretty much every subjectivist theory on offer will imply that Bundy was very well-off. But some have the reaction that it is not possible for Bundy's own attitudes, no matter how positive they are, to turn his way of life into a desirable one in any way, including the well-being way.

It must be admitted that some objectivists will have to say some positive things about Bundy's way of life too, such as those objectivists who find basic prudential value in the development of one's abilities (Parfit), autonomy (Griffin), enjoyment (Griffin), or practical reason (Nussbaum). There is no reason to think that Bundy lacked these putative goods. Many of the values on Frankena's initial list could easily find instantiation in a Bundy-like life, too: activity, health, strength, pleasures and satisfactions, contentment, knowledge and true opinion of various kinds, aesthetic experience, power and experiences of achievement, self-expression, freedom, adventure, and novelty.

If an objectivist is going to be able to rate Bundy's life low in welfare, it will help to have items like the following on one's list: deep personal relations (Griffin); emotional attachment (Nussbaum); wisdom, mutual affection, love, friendship (Frankena); and, especially, morally good dispositions or virtues, good reputation, honor, and esteem (Frankena). One important tool available to objectivists is the ability to say that so many of the would-be subjective goods in Bundy's life – his enjoyments, desire satisfactions, aim achievements, and so forth, which objectivists can admit are typically important prudential goods – are completely defeated by the fact that the objects of these enjoyments, desires, and aims were immoral. Objectivists can say that enjoyment and desire satisfaction are typically basically good things to get, but that they fail to be good – and may even be positively bad – when they are directed at immoral or otherwise unworthy objects. This strategy may go far, but it should be admitted by objectivists that whether Bundy had a good or bad life *overall*, welfare-wise, will be a matter of how the various goods he receives weigh against the various ills.

Other sorts of life are filled with desires and pleasures whose objects, while not positively immoral, seem nevertheless pointless or stupid. Although he is a subjectivist unbothered by the case, the philosopher John Rawls famously

> imagine[s] someone whose only pleasure is to count blades of grass in various geometrically shaped areas such as park squares and well-trimmed lawns. He is otherwise intelligent and actually possesses unusual skills, since he manages to survive by solving difficult mathematical problems for a fee. The definition of the good [that Rawls endorses] forces us to admit that the good for this man is indeed counting blades of grass. (Rawls 1971: 432)

But an objectivist who believes in the value of things such as achievement, friendship, honor, adventure, and novelty has resources to judge the grass counter's life to be lacking in significant prudentially relevant respects.

One subjectivist reply to cases of immoral and pointless desires begins with a reminder of the important distinctions among ways lives can be evaluated. In

Section 1, we noted that in addition to judging lives prudentially, we judge them morally as well. The subjectivist will agree that when fair-minded people consider Bundy's life, they will judge that something is indeed amiss with it. But this vague intuition of "something being amiss" is an intuition that subjectivism about well-being can accommodate, for the subjectivist can agree that Bundy's life is *morally* amiss. And that may be enough to do justice to our negative assessment of Bundy's life, to our refusal to encourage his way of life in our children, and so forth.

The subjectivist can say something similar about Rawls's grass counter, noting that his life ranks poorly with respect to *meaning*. Although the grass counter's life seems pretty much meaningless, this is not to say that he isn't benefitting from his meaningless existence.

Adaptive Preferences. Another challenge that can make objectivism look more attractive is the problem of adaptive preferences. The philosopher Wayne Sumner describes it as "the main reason for questioning the adequacy of any subjective theory of welfare, whatever its constituent ingredients, and for favouring more objective accounts" (Sumner 1996: 162). Imagine a person whose hopes and dreams are invariably crushed, whose day-to-day needs and desires are rarely met, and whose daily burdens and irritations never diminish. Eventually, he gives up on his hopes and dreams and resigns himself to the sorry state of his life; rather than continuing to try to adapt his situation to his preferences, he adapts his preferences to his situation.

Subjectivists seem committed to looking on this as an excellent way of dealing with the situation. The preference adapter is now able to get all they want out of life. But this may seem like a problem for subjectivism, because the whole situation still seems rather unfortunate. To have to adapt one's preferences in this way rather than being able to get what one really wanted – surely this is not ideal.

The putative problem for subjectivism is described by economist Amartya Sen, one of the problem's champions:

> A person who has had a life of misfortune, with very little opportunities, and rather little hope, may be more easily reconciled to deprivations than others reared in more fortunate and affluent circumstances. The metric of happiness may, therefore, distort the extent of deprivation, in a specific and biased way. The hopeless beggar, the precarious landless labourer, the dominated house-wife, the hardened unemployed or the over-exhausted coolie may all take pleasures in small mercies, and manage to suppress intense suffering for the necessity of continuing survival, but it would be ethically deeply mistaken to attach a correspondingly small value to the loss of their well-being because of this survival strategy. The same problem arises with the other interpretation

of utility, namely, desire-fulfilment, since the hopelessly deprived lack the courage to desire much, and their deprivations are muted and deadened in the scale of desire-fulfilment. (Sen 1987: 45–6)

The problem of adaptive preferences causes thinkers like Sen and Martha Nussbaum to prefer an objective theory of well-being. Recall some of Nussbaum's list: life, health, bodily integrity, emotional attachment, play. Those living in what anyone would describe as unfortunate circumstances may get themselves to stop caring about any of Nussbaum's goods and learn to have no complaints about a life that is short, diseased, disabled, detached, and laborious. If it seems better to you to instead have a life filled with longevity, health, bodily integrity, emotional attachment, and play – *no matter what you want, like, or care about* – then you can see the appeal of objectivism here.

The problem of adaptive preferences is a complicated topic, but we can note some elements of a possible subjectivist reply. First, subjectivists can recognize the prudential value of some of the items in Nussbaum's list even, surprisingly, for those who don't care about them. To illustrate, subjectivists can agree that longevity is typically an important prudential good even for those who have no positive attitudes toward longevity; that's because the longer you live, the more pro-attitude satisfaction you can accumulate (making longevity an important *instrumental* prudential good by subjectivist lights).

Second, subjectivists can deliver the results that Sen and Nussbaum want about *real-life* cases. Just about any normal person, if he moves from being a beggar to having stable employment, will get a better life by subjectivist lights – and this even if he managed to adapt fairly well to the life of a beggar. This is because it is practically impossible to get oneself to be *completely* unbothered by such a life. How actual, typical people feel in such cases is important because Sen and Nussbaum are especially concerned with how these subjectivist theories will affect real-world public policy.

Finally, consider Sen's claim that the "hopelessly deprived lack the courage to desire much." If this is true, then the hopelessly deprived will tend to get worse lives even by the lights of the desire-satisfaction theory. The desire-satisfaction theory implies that if the hopelessly deprived were to get into a better situation – one in which they desired more and got it – then they would be getting better lives.

Babies. Philosopher Richard Kraut argues that subjectivism goes wrong when it comes to human infants:

there is no plausibility in the idea that a baby's good can be constructed out of what she wants. Babies must, for their own good, be nurtured in a way that gives them certain competencies and brings them into certain human relationships; but the states of affairs that are good for them are not already present to them as the content of their desires. (Kraut 2007: 105)

As an example, Kraut cites the fact that it is good for a baby to start learning a language as soon as they can even though, being a baby, they have no desire to learn a language (Kraut 2007: 106). Kraut's challenge here makes trouble for some forms of subjectivism, but not all. We'll be in a better position to explain this later.

Challenges to Objectivist Views

Let's now move on to problems for objectivism. We have already seen what I regard as its central challenge: its incompatibility with the resonance constraint. In addition to this general challenge to objectivism, there are objections specific to objectivism's two main varieties, objective-list theory and perfectionism.

An Explanatory Challenge for Objective-List Theory. One challenge to object-ive-list theory is an explanatory one. Because any objective-list theory puts forth a plurality of goods, it is natural to ask: Why this list?

I don't think it is possible for an objective-list theorist to answer this question without abandoning their theory. Suppose we have an objective-list theory that puts forth five goods. The objection is asking for an explanation of the fact that just these five things are the basic goods. The natural way to answer this would be to find some more general good under which to subsume the five goods. But to do this would simply be to abandon the idea that these five goods are the *basic* goods; the more general good would be the sole basic good instead.

Is it a problem that the objective-list theory cannot explain why just the goods that it posits are the basic goods? In my view, no. The objective-list theorist should say that there simply is no explanation of the fact that just these five things are the basic goods; this is simply one of the fundamental facts of value theory, and that's that. If this sounds unpalatable, note that monist theories (including subjectivist theories) face essentially the same problem. Hedonists hold that there is just one basic good: pleasure. We can ask hedonists for an explanation of the fact that pleasure is the sole basic good. But if hedonists were to have an answer for this – for example, if they were to say that the ability to experience pleasure is the most central facet of human nature and exercising the most central facet of our nature is the sole basic good – then they would be abandoning hedonism (in this case, for perfectionism). Hedonists should say instead that there simply is no explanation of the fact that just this one thing (pleasure) is the basic good. This is simply one of the fundamental facts of value theory, and that's that.

Objective-List Theory and Incomparability. A second objection specific to the objective-list theory also targets its pluralism. Theories of well-being are supposed to tell us *how good* any good thing is, as well as how to compute the value of larger wholes that contain various goods, such as someone's day, childhood, or whole life. Doing the last requires being able to compare instances of different goods with respect to their basic prudential value. If they are instances of the same good – for example, all states of pleasure – this seems doable. The basic prudential value of an instance of pleasure is equal to its magnitude, which is itself a function of the pleasure's intensity and duration. And different pleasures can be compared with respect to their magnitude, at least in principle.

But how do we compare the prudential value of a pleasure with the prudential value of, say, a state of understanding (a thing that might appear on an objective list)? There is no sense to be made of the claim that the magnitude of the state of pleasure might be greater than, less than, or equal to the magnitude of the state of understanding. Some philosophers have thought that, because of this, there is likewise no sense to be made of the claim that the *prudential value* of the state of pleasure might be greater than, less than, or equal to that of the state of understanding. If this is the case, then these two states are said to be "incomparable" with respect to prudential value. If this holds generally for any two very different prudential goods, then objective-list theories cannot say how such goods compare prudentially, and they cannot say what the prudential value is of some larger whole containing instances of both goods. There simply will be no such facts of the matter on this picture.

The argument here aims to establish the implausibility of objective-list theories from these two premises: that objective-list theories are committed to this sort of incomparability in prudential value; and that theories that are so committed are implausible.

But both premises are open to doubt. If pleasure and understanding are basic prudential goods, then any instance of either of them will be good in itself for the person getting it. Since each one will be good in this way, there must be some extent to which it is good in that way. How could a thing be good in some way but there be no extent to which it is good in that way? This extent or magnitude will, it would seem, be a common currency in terms of which the two goods can be compared. In this way, it seems that prudential value incomparability is simply not possible.

The main reason to think that prudential value incomparability nevertheless does occur is that, for some pairs of prudential goods, we are at a loss as to how to compare them. But this isn't true for all such pairs. On the assumption that both pleasure and understanding are basic prudential goods, I am confident that the value of the pleasure that I get from a single lick of a lollipop is less than the value of my fully understanding quantum mechanics for the rest of my life. Similarly, the value of the pleasure I got spending a snow day with my friends in graduate school (one of the most enjoyable days of my life) is greater than the value of understanding somewhat, for a few moments, why a certain student was late to class. Since some instances of pleasure can be compared in terms of prudential value with some instances of understanding, there is at least nothing in the nature of these two goods that makes them incomparable. Perhaps, then, when we are at a loss as to how to compare other pairs of instances of them, this is due merely to our ignorance of their relative value rather than to there being no fact of the matter.

But suppose you are not convinced by this and you think that many instances of pleasure and understanding are incomparable in value. Why then, as the second premise above claims, should this be any reason to think that pleasure and understanding are not basic goods? Why not instead think that this is apparently just how evaluative reality is, and so an objective-list theory that reflects these strange facets of it, by including value incomparability in the theory, is just doing its job?

Challenges to Perfectionism. Perfectionism, recall, is the view that what is basically good for us is the development of those traits and capacities that are a part of human nature. Because perfectionism is a form of monism – it puts forth just *one* basic good for us, *the development of traits that are a part of human nature* – the objections above to the objective-list theory do not arise. But perfectionist theories face their own challenges.

The main dimension along which perfectionist theories differ is with regards to their accounts of human nature. On one simple interpretation of Aristotle, he suggests that we flourish when we develop those traits that are distinctive of human beings – that is, that are *unique* to us (*Nicomachean Ethics* I.7). And Aristotle thought that it is our rationality that sets us apart.

But this Aristotelian approach has this odd feature: it makes our well-being dependent on whether there happen to be other rational beings in the universe. Surely how good our lives are for us does not constitutively depend on that. Another problem is that there are some human traits that are unique to us that are pretty clearly prudentially irrelevant. Evidently, humans are the only creatures who sweat by secreting water onto the surface of their skin and who cry tears of emotion. But it is not plausible to think that we thrive only when we have developed these traits to their fullest.

Other perfectionists maintain that our nature consists of those traits that are *essential* to humans. These are the traits that you must have if you are to count as a human being at all. Advocates of this approach might want to say that the traits that are essential to being human are traits like rationality, autonomy, sociality, and emotionality.

Such traits might form the basis of a promising form of perfectionism, but it is not plausible that such traits are essential to being human. In fact, some human beings lack all of them; recall Giles, the unfortunate human in a coma. Moreover, other traits that are more clearly essential to being human seem to be of no prudential relevance. Consider the fact that you cannot be human unless you are *extended in space*. We can reject out of hand a theory of well-being that says that you are better off the more space you take up.

A third approach holds that perfectionists should appeal to those traits that are *characteristic* of humans in the sense of being typical of human beings and representative of them. This conception of human nature does yield some traits that it seems good to have and to develop – rationality, autonomy, sociality, compassion, loyalty, curiosity – but there is no getting around the fact that many negative traits also define us. Perfectionists don't want to have to say that we live the best lives that we can when we develop the human tendencies to be tribal, hateful, lazy, insecure, jealous, vengeful, and vain.

Although this does not exhaust the perfectionist's options, it casts doubt on the initially attractive guiding idea that our lives are better the more fully human they are.[3] Due to the challenges of grounding well-being in human nature, some who identify as perfectionists simply list those human characteristics that they think it is good for us to develop. They might call them "human excellences." But if these traits are put forth simply because they are intuitively prudentially valuable rather than because they are derived from human nature, then this is not perfectionism but objective-list theory.

Matters of Mere Taste. The last challenge to objectivism that we'll consider is a problem only for "extreme" versions of objectivism, that is, versions that include no subjective goods. The problem is that it seems that at least some welfare goods are subjective; that is, for at least some pro-attitude, the mere satisfaction of it or the having of it toward something with no independent value in itself is directly beneficial.

This modest thesis is hard to resist when one considers *matters of mere taste*. Suppose that both Ina and Lulu are craving a beer. The bar has an IPA and a lager on tap. Ina loves the bold hoppiness of an IPA and finds lager watery and bland. But IPAs are too bitter for Lulu's palate; she prefers the crispness and drinkability of a lager. Side-effects aside, it is obvious that Ina will benefit more if she gets to drink the IPA and Lulu the lager. But there is little plausibility to the claim that

---

[3] For readers interested in pursuing more sophisticated perfectionist options than I consider here, see Shields 2014, Hurka 1993, and Kitcher 1999.

some beers – and, more generally, some taste sensations – are *objectively* tastier and better than others. This suggests that at least some welfare goods are pro-attitude-involving.[4]

2.5 The Hybrid Theory

The preceding discussion gives us a sense of the debate between objectivism and subjectivism about well-being. If you find yourself pulled in both directions, there is a middle way. Derek Parfit introduces a view of well-being that combines what he thinks is appealing in the two rival approaches:

> We might . . . claim that what is best for people is a composite. It is not just their being in the conscious states that they want to be in [as a subjectivist might say]. Nor is it just their having knowledge, engaging in rational activity, being aware of true beauty, and the like [as an objectivist might say]. What is good for someone . . . is to have knowledge, to be engaged in rational activity, to experience mutual love, and to be aware of beauty, while strongly wanting just these things. On this view, each side in this disagreement saw only half of the truth. Each put forward as sufficient something that was only necessary. Pleasure with many other kinds of object has no value. And, if they are entirely devoid of pleasure, there is no value in knowledge, rational activity, love, or the awareness of beauty. What is of value, or is good for someone, is to have both; to be engaged in these activities, and to be strongly wanting to be so engaged. (Parfit 1984: 502)

Parfit is here describing what is known as the *hybrid theory* of well-being. Whereas a subjectivist might hold that well-being consists in the having of a certain favorable attitude toward whatever you like, a hybrid theorist would hold that it must be had toward *the right things*, things that meet some objective standard.

The theory Parfit sketches simply lists the acceptable objects of the favorable attitude, but other views offer a unified standard. Philosopher Robert Adams holds that well-being amounts ("primarily") to enjoying what is objectively excellent. Excellence is "the type of goodness exemplified by the beauty of a sunset, a painting, or a mathematical proof, or by the greatness of a novel, the nobility of an unselfish deed, or the quality of an athletic or a philosophical performance" (Adams 1999: 83). Since both enjoyment and excellence come in degrees, the most natural way to formulate views with this structure is to have the prudential value of a state of enjoying something excellent equal the mathematical product of the amount of enjoyment taken in the object and the amount of excellence in the object.

---

[4] This argument fails if a sensation-based theory of sensory pleasure is true; these are discussed in Section 4. The use of the phrase "matters of mere taste" in this context is due to Sobel (2005).

The hybrid theory is in fact quite old. The ancient Roman philosopher Cicero is reported to have held that "to will what is not fitting, is itself most miserable" (Augustine 416: ch. 5). This suggests a view with structural similarities to Adams's on which what is good for us is to successfully will that which it is fitting or appropriate to will. Unselfish deeds are presumably fit to be willed, whereas acts of cruelty are not.

Views with this structure are the paradigm hybrid theory, but we can imagine more relaxed hybrid theories that impose only a negative standard on the object of the pro-attitude. The having of the favorable attitude is prudentially good as long as its object is not something positively bad, such as the suffering of another. This close-but-not-quite-subjectivist theory would let all manner of trivial pleasures and cheap thrills count. The medieval philosopher St. Augustine may have been endorsing a view of this sort when he wrote that "he only is a blessed man, who both has all things which he wills, and wills nothing ill" (Augustine 416: ch. 5).

2.5.1 Evaluating the Hybrid Theory

The Hybrid Theory and the Resonance Constraint

The most important advantage that the hybrid theory has over objectivism about well-being is that it obeys our old friend the

Resonance Constraint: A thing, x, is basically good for some subject, S, only if either S has a satisfied positive attitude toward x or x itself involves S's having a satisfied positive attitude toward something.

This is because hybrid theories hold that the basic well-being states are states in which some subject has a positive attitude toward something. Hybrid theories conform to the intuition that you aren't being benefitted in some situation if you are left completely cold in that situation.

This is good news for hybrid theories, but I believe that a related problem remains. Hybrid theories can accommodate the idea that there is benefit on the scene only if there is a favorable attitude on the scene, but they cannot accommodate the following similar idea: that a person receives *more* benefit in some situation (than she would receive in some alternative possible situation) only if she receives *more* favorable-attitude satisfaction or has a stronger favorable attitude in that situation (than she would receive or have in that alternative possible situation). The resonance constraint says, roughly, "x is good only if x resonates"; this new constraint says "x is *better* only if x resonates *more*." Because this new constraint is saying that we have a greater amount of good only if we have a greater amount of resonance, we can call it the *greater resonance constraint*.

Suppose you are taking your niece out for her birthday, and you want to give her the best night that you can – not the morally best, the most meaningful, or the most edifying, but the night that would be most in her interest to get. You could take her to a Tokyo Jetz concert, which she would love every minute of, or to a Yo-Yo Ma concert, which she would enjoy pretty well, but definitely not as much. Suppose all else is equal (so that, for example, taking her to the Yo-Yo Ma concert wouldn't spark a love for the cello from which your niece would derive great satisfaction later on). It seems that you would give your niece a better night for her if you took her to Tokyo Jetz rather than Yo-Yo Ma.

But paradigm versions of the hybrid theory, such as an enjoyment-of-the-excellent theory, conflict with this judgment, provided that we fill out the example in the right way. If we assume that the music of Tokyo Jetz is less excellent than that of Yo-Yo Ma by a sufficient degree, then this theory will imply that you would give your niece a better evening by taking her to Yo-Yo Ma, in spite of the fact that she'd enjoy Tokyo Jetz more and that the increased excellence of Yo-Yo Ma would leave her cold.

This example also serves to illustrate how paradigm hybrid theories violate the greater resonance constraint. The Tokyo Jetz concert would resonate more with your niece than would the Yo-Yo Ma concert, but (given certain reasonable auxiliary claims) these hybrid theories imply that the Yo-Yo Ma concert would nevertheless be more beneficial.

The more relaxed hybrid theory, the sort that imposes only a negative stand-ard, can avoid this counterexample if it denies that Tokyo Jetz is positively bad in the way relevant to the theory. The theory might, for example, claim that only *moral* badness has the ability to undermine the prudential value of enjoyment or desire satisfaction. But we could imagine a variation on the case. Suppose what your niece would most love to do on her birthday happens to be something morally objectionable, such as attend a cockfight. My own view at least is that she would get a better night prudentially (although, of course, not morally) if she were to do that than if she were to see Yo-Yo Ma. If you balk at this judgment, recall Korva, the meat-loving college student whom we judged would benefit more if she continued eating meat – even on the assumption that there are strong moral reasons against doing so.

It seems to me, then, that, although hybrid theories do better with respect to issues of resonance than do objective theories, they still may not do well enough.

The Hybrid Theory and Matters of Mere Taste

Matters of mere taste suggest that any theory of well-being should include wholly subjective goods. Hybrid theories effectively do this if they feature only a negative standard. It's a good thing for Ina when she enjoys her IPA, and she has more reason to order the IPA than the lager. Since neither IPA nor lager is objectively bad, relaxed hybrid views treat this case as subjectivist views do. However, since, I take it, no taste sensations are objectively good or excellent, the paradigm hybrid theories seem unable to say that it's a good thing for Ina when she enjoys her IPA, nor that she has more prudential reason to order it over the lager. That seems like a serious strike against the paradigm hybrid views.

Hybrid Theories and Defective Interests

We saw that a possible problem for subjectivism is that, when it comes to the things a person could be into, there are no rules. No matter how immoral or stupid it is, if you like it, it is good for you. Subjectivists tend not to be too bothered by this, but if it bothers you, hybrid theories offer different ways out while allowing the subject's likes and cares still to play an important role in shaping their welfare. A relaxed, merely-negative-standard hybrid view can deem worthless all of Bundy's malicious pleasures and desire satisfactions. It may not deliver the result that Bundy's life was worthless, but it can deliver the result that he would have had a better life if much of the things he liked to do and got to do were not horribly immoral.

The relaxed hybrid view would seem to have to agree with the subjectivist, however, about the life of Rawls's grass counter, since there is nothing positively bad, I assume, about counting blades of grass. The more stringent kind of hybrid theory, however, can rate the life of the grass counter very poorly, since this is not an activity that manifests excellence or is fit to be desired. But recall how matters of mere taste suggest that this view seems *too* stringent.

Hybrid Theories and Adaptive Preferences

If I am living a life of poverty, tedious labor, and loneliness, subjective theories seem to imply that it would be no better for me to satisfy my present desires for financial security, rewarding work, and a rich social life than to learn to love the poverty, the tedious labor, and the loneliness. Objective theories that hold that financial security, rewarding work, and a rich social life are objectively prudentially valuable, and that poverty, tedious labor, and loneliness are objectively against anyone's interests, avoid this implication. Hybrid theories can also avoid it.

If financial security, rewarding work, and a rich social life are favored by the hybrid theory (say by being fitting to desire, or by their alternatives being objectively bad) then the hybrid theory can deliver the result that it would be better for me to satisfy my present desires for financial security, rewarding work, and a rich social life than to learn to love the poverty, tedious labor, and loneliness. The hybrid theory, then, appears to do just as well at avoiding the problem of adaptive preference as fully objective theories do.

2.6 Concluding Remarks

No issue in the theory of well-being is more fundamental than the question of whether well-being is objective, subjective, or a hybrid of the two. Subjectivism is the only theory that does full justice to resonance-related intuitions, but hybrid theories do better by them than do objective theories. As we have seen above, however, objective theories may have other advantages. I leave it to the reader to come to their own view on this most crucial issue in the theory of well-being.

Does it matter, in practice, or for the purposes of policy, whether an objective or a subjective theory of well-being is true? Not really. The reason is that the goods on objective theories are things that most people enjoy and want in their lives anyway. This means that objective and subjective theories will tend to agree about which lives are better or worse than which other lives, and about which actions or policies will tend to make some person or population better or worse off. Subjectivists might even offer an interesting explanation of this agreement: they might say that, in declaring certain things objectively prudentially good, objectivists are, without knowing it, simply projecting and "objectifying" their own tastes.

To be sure, objectivists and subjectivists will still disagree over the ultimate *explanation* as to why some act or policy would be worth choosing. Ultimate explanations are what philosophers tend to traffic in, even when doing so has no practical upshot. The subjectivist will say that the policy is worth choosing because in choosing it we would (say) be giving the people what they want; the objectivist might say that it is because we would be giving people something that is objectively worth wanting.

3 The Nature of Happiness

The last section was all about well-being and theories of it. We characterized a crucial distinction among such theories: objective vs. subjective. Among the varieties of subjective theory mentioned was the *happiness theory*, the view that the single basic good is happiness. The present section is devoted to this putative good. Our question is the most fundamental question one can ask about happiness: what is it?

We can ask the same question about any putative good: knowledge, achievement, pleasure, desire satisfaction, virtue, friendship. A complete treatment of the topic of well-being, if there could ever be one, would want to address, for each of these putative goods, that same fundamental question: what exactly is it? We won't have the space to do that in this Element, but we will do it for happiness (and also for pleasure, in Section 4).

It makes sense to prioritize examining happiness. One reason is that it may be the most intuitively compelling example of a human prudential good, perhaps even more compelling an example than pleasure, which can have an air of unseemliness about it. If we can't discuss the nature of all of the minimally plausible putative prudential goods, we should at least discuss the nature of the most compelling one or two. Another reason is that some people think it might be something of a tautology that the good life is the happy life. They think that when we ask what makes people better off we *just are* asking what makes people happy. Evaluating this idea requires inquiring into the nature of happiness.

An inquiry into the nature of happiness, our topic here, is not an inquiry into the principal *causes* or *sources* of happiness. Claims about the sources of happiness are sometimes colloquially expressed using the expression "happiness is _____," a phrase that can also be used to express views about the nature of happiness. Thus, one might hear that happiness is a warm puppy, or a warm gun. Warm puppies and warm guns may be reliable sources of happiness, but they are not plausible candidates for what constitutes happiness. This Element, as a work of philosophy rather than science, is concerned with this constitutive question rather than the causal question.

This news may be disappointing. It is more practically useful and ethically valuable to learn how to increase happiness, in yourself and in others, than it is to learn what happiness is. Thankfully, there is no shortage of advice on how to promote happiness.[5]

3.1 Phenomena that Travel Under the Label "Happiness"

In Section 1, we noted that the term "happy" is ambiguous. Several distinct phenomena go by that name. Three such phenomena will be our focus.

Episodic Happiness. Although he doesn't use this term for it, the philosopher Wayne Davis has a nice characterization of episodic happiness:

> In the [episodic] sense, "*A* is happy" means that *A* feels happy or is *experiencing* happiness; he is in high or good spirits, is in a good mood, and feels

---

[5] The interested reader might begin with section ten of David et al. 2013, or, what is perhaps more effective, Gay 2019.

good … That someone is smiling, has sparkling eyes, looks healthy and rested, and is bubbling effusively about a favorite hobby is good evidence of [episodic] happiness. (Davis 1981b: 305)

We use this sense all the time. If your roommate strolls in with a huge grin on his face, you might ask: "What are you so happy about?" Or if your dog wags his tail vigorously when your sister shows up, you might say exclaim: "I can't believe how happy he gets every time you come over!" In either case, you'd be making use of perhaps the most familiar notion of happiness. We'll call it "episodic happiness" (following Raibley 2012) because it comes in these discrete episodes.

Happiness in Life. But other times, when we say that a person is happy, we don't have in mind single, discrete episodes like this but something apparently deeper, or something more. A friend you haven't seen in a long time catches you up on her life; it prompts you to ask: "OK, but are you *happy*?" Here you are not asking her to say whether she is at that moment experiencing happiness, as your roommate and dog were above. You seem to be asking her about something more general.

I'm not sure what the best term for it is, but I'll follow Elizabeth Telfer in using "happiness in life" (Telfer 1980: 1). Wayne Sumner uses "having a happy life" or simply "being happy" for this phenomenon (Sumner 1996: 145); although, for the latter option, it may better convey the change in meaning if we italicize the key word, as I did in the previous paragraph. Also grasping at a notion of happiness somehow deeper than episodic happiness, Julia Annas observes that "we do talk about happiness over our lives as wholes, or at least over long stretches of them. We should not, then, restrict talk of happiness at the start to contexts of short-term feeling" (Annas 2004: 45).

We regularly employ this notion in ordinary life too, as in the following familiar sorts of remark: "I had a happy childhood"; "I didn't realize it until now, but I've been unhappy for some time"; "When you were married to him, were you happy?"; "You should choose the career that will make you happiest."

Dispositional Happiness. When we are concerned with happiness, sometimes we are concerned with something more ingrained in those who have it than either episodic happiness or happiness in life need be. We can call this having of a happy temperament *dispositional happiness*. The clearest way for a person to be dispositionally happy is for her to have an underlying tendency to experience episodic happiness.

We employ the concept of dispositional happiness in ordinary language and thought too, but I think that, rather than with the simple predicate "is happy," it is more clearly expressed with a predicate of the form "is a happy ___," as in "is a happy person" or "is a happy dog."

Consider finally the notion of *being in a good mood*. This notion seems to sit somewhere near the border between episodic and dispositional happiness. The Davis passage above suggests that he sees it as a form or element of episodic happiness. But other philosophers, such as Robert Nozick, assimilate it with dispositional happiness and describe a happy mood as "the proneness or tendency to have and feel [certain other] types of happiness emotions" (Nozick 1989: 114).

The goal of this section is to explore the leading accounts of the nature of these various happiness phenomena.

3.2 Hedonism about Happiness

"Utilitarianism" is the name of a doctrine about right and wrong; it holds roughly that the right act in any situation is the one that best promotes total well-being. The great British utilitarians – Jeremy Bentham, John Stuart Mill, Henry Sidgwick – all endorsed hedonism about well-being, which, recall, is the view that pleasure is the single basic welfare good and pain the single basic bad. They were also hedonists about happiness:

> The business of government is to promote the happiness of society ... What happiness consists of we have already seen: enjoyment of pleasures, security from pains. (Bentham 1789: ch. VII)

> [T]he Greatest Happiness Principle ... holds that actions are right in proportion as they tend to promote happiness, wrong as they tend to produce the reverse of happiness. By happiness is intended pleasure, and the absence of pain; by unhappiness, pain, and the privation of pleasure. (Mill 1863: 9–10)

> We shall understand ... that by Greatest Happiness is meant the greatest possible surplus of pleasure over pain, the pain being conceived as balanced against an equal amount of pleasure, so that the two contrasted amounts annihilate each other for purposes of ethical calculation. (Sidgwick 1907: 413)

Bentham, Mill, and Sidgwick were hedonists about both episodic happiness and happiness in life, understanding the latter as simply an aggregation of the former. We can state their account as follows:

Hedonism about Happiness:
(i) (a) Episodic happiness is simply pleasure: experiencing an episode of happiness (or unhappiness) is the same thing as experiencing an episode of pleasure (or pain); (b) The amount of episodic happiness (or

unhappiness) in an episode of happiness (or unhappiness) is equal to the amount of pleasure (or pain) in it.

(ii) To be *happy* – that is, to have happiness in life – is to experience more pleasure than pain in your life; to be *unhappy* is to experience more pain than pleasure in your life.

(iii) To be dispositionally happy is to be prone to experiencing pleasure and not so much pain; to be dispositionally unhappy is to be prone to experiencing pain and not so much pleasure.

We'll have more to say about pleasure in the next section, but for now it is useful to note that there are at least two kinds of pleasure. There is *sensory pleasure*, which many of us experience when we receive the pressure sensations of a neck massage or experience the sweet tingling taste of drinking a Coca-Cola. There is also *attitudinal pleasure*, which is more intellectual; it is what one experiences when one is pleased that something is the case. Right now, I am pleased that I am getting some writing in today, that my dog is lying next to me, and that it is sunny outside. Sometimes we overlook attitudinal pleasure and think only of sensory pleasure when we think of pleasure. That makes hedonism about happiness seem less plausible. For, pre-theoretically, happiness seems more like an attitude than a sensation. But if we keep in mind that pleasure includes attitudinal pleasure, hedonism about happiness should seem like a theory worth considering (Feldman 2010).

Very much worth considering is the *general kind* of account that hedonism gives of happiness in life. This is the idea that happiness in life – being *happy* – is to be understood simply in terms of aggregate episodic happiness. This aggregation idea can be endorsed whatever one's view of episodic happiness, whether hedonistic or something else. Its advocates hope to capture the seeming greater depth and importance of happiness in life by appeal to the fact that, on this view, happiness in life is a kind of catalog or full accounting of all of the episodic happiness and unhappiness in a life.

A common way of measuring happiness fits well with hedonism. Scientists have devised all sorts of ways to measure happiness, from ratings based on interviews with subjects, to asking subjects' family and friends how happy they are, to seeing how often subjects smile. But the most common way is simply to ask subjects directly. This self-report approach comes in two main varieties: *global* and *moment-based*. Global instruments ask for the subject's own evaluation of their life as a whole; moment-based approaches, also known as "experience sampling," prompt subjects at random times throughout the day to rate how they are feeling at that moment. If hedonism is the correct theory of the nature of happiness, then the moment-based approach is better. Many subjects, when evaluating their life globally, will take into account more than just how pleasant their life is. And even for those who judge their lives solely on this basis, they may not have an accurate picture of how pleasant or unpleasant their lives are. Experience sampling, by contrast, asks subjects how they are feeling at the moment. This is a better basis on which to infer how much pleasure or pain the subject is feeling at the moment, which is the hedonist's conception of episodic happiness. It is also a better basis on which to know about happiness in life on the hedonist's conception; this would be determined not by asking the subject about their aggregate pleasure and pain but by having the researcher aggregate it themselves, from the moment-by-moment data.

3.2.1 Objections to Hedonism about Happiness

Of course, hedonism has been subject to criticism. One interesting line of attack aims to show that hedonism doesn't do justice to our interest in happiness, or to the idea that happiness is important. Crediting the objection to Daniel Haybron, philosopher Mauro Rossi writes:

> When we care about happiness, we seem to care about something more than a series of experiences. We seem to care about a more robust mental state, something that can have a profound impact on the individual's life, something akin to a psychological condition. (Rossi 2018: 900)

Because hedonism as we have formulated it holds that happiness in life is indeed a mere aggregate of experiences, we can see this objection as targeting hedonism's view about happiness in life.

But hedonism is able to accommodate the thought that happiness is something more like a robust psychological condition than a mere series of experiences. This is because one kind of happiness that hedonism recognizes and accounts for is dispositional happiness, and, on hedonism, dispositional happiness *is* something more robust than a mere series of experiences. It is an underlying tendency to have such experiences. Presumably such dispositions are typically fairly durable, or "robust." Thus the hedonist can agree that when we care about happiness, we are often caring about a more robust mental state, one that can have a profound impact on one's life, one akin to a psychological condition.

In responding in this way on behalf of the hedonist, am I implying that the hedonist should say that only dispositional happiness is worth caring about? No. The hedonist can say that episodic happiness and its aggregate in a life are also important. Moreover, the value of dispositional happiness, which is what the hedonist should say the objector above is thinking about, is, it would seem, parasitic on the value of episodic happiness. Dispositional happiness would seem to be of mere derivative value: it's good to have it only because episodic happiness is good to have and dispositional happiness helps you get it. If we imagine a person who has a robust inbuilt disposition to experience episodic happiness, but, through endless bad luck, never gets to experience any, we are imagining someone who is not benefitting from his disposition to be happy.

But Haybron has a better objection to hedonism:

> The most obvious problem with traditional hedonistic theories is that they are too inclusive: all sorts of shallow, fleeting pleasures are made to count toward happiness. Yet such pleasures intuitively play no constitutive role in determining how happy a person is. One's enjoyment of [say] eating crackers ... need not have the slightest impact on one's level of happiness. (Haybron 2008: 63)

Suppose you are in a neutral state of mind. You take a bite of a saltine cracker and experience the pleasant, salty crunch. So you experience some pleasure. Does it follow that you also experienced some happiness?

I'm inclined to say no, it doesn't follow. You *could* be happy, for some reason, that you are getting this cracker, or about something else. But, contrary to what hedonism implies, you need not get any happiness when you get the cracker pleasure. This, which Haybron calls the problem of irrelevant pleasures, strikes me as a persuasive counterexample to hedonism's view of episodic happiness.

Some hedonists bite the bullet and insist that the cracker pleasure is itself an experience of happiness (Feldman 2010: 27–8). One thing they might say to defend this is that, in considering this case, we overlook the cracker happiness because it is so mild. But, as Haybron himself notes, even intense pleasures and pains can fail to constitute experiences of happiness or unhappiness. Someone who occasionally experiences brief but intense headaches, and has learned not to get wrapped up in the pain, might get a truly intense pain without experiencing any unhappiness.

Let's consider a third and final objection to hedonism about happiness. Recall what we did above to get across the concept of happiness in life. We supposed that a friend you hadn't seen in a long time catches you up on her life, and it makes you ask: "OK, but are you *happy*?" We know hedonism's account of this notion: when you ask your friend "OK, but are you *happy*?," you are, whether you realize it or not, asking her whether she is experiencing more pleasure than pain in her life. But imagine that your friend answers: "Yes, I've been enjoying myself thoroughly." In response to this, one could imagine your saying the following: "I get that you're enjoying yourself, but what I want to know is whether you're *happy*."

It might seem that you are on to something with this remark. Perhaps you are on to a concept of happiness that is not constituted merely by an aggregation of states of pleasure and pain in a person's life, or even by an aggregation of episodic happiness and unhappiness, whatever that amounts to. What, then, might you have in mind if you were to say this? Perhaps you'd have in mind something to do with how your friend would assess her life. If, rather than a mere aggregation of episodic happiness, happiness in life is something more like that, then, even if hedonism's account of episodic happiness is correct, its account of happiness in life cannot be.

3.3 The Whole-Life-Satisfaction Theory of Happiness

Hedonism tends to be the theory of happiness accepted by the philosophers whose moral theories enshrine the concept of happiness (the utilitarians). Perhaps influenced partly by the idea that happiness must be something deeper than mere pleasure and partly by how happiness tends to be measured, many scientists and philosophers nowadays accept a different view: the whole-life-satisfaction theory of happiness. Whereas hedonists hold, in a word, that happiness is pleasure, whole-life satisfactionists hold that happiness is satisfaction with one's life as a whole.

These remarks make it seem as if hedonism and whole-life satisfactionism are straightforward competitors, and it is standard in the philosophy of happiness to treat them this way; but I think matters aren't quite so simple. Recall that one paradigm example of episodic happiness is of your dog wagging his tail with gusto when your sister comes over. This shows that whatever episodic happiness consists in, we can be confident that it is not *satisfaction with one's life as a whole*. For, in this example, your dog is happy, but he is not satisfied with his life as a whole. Nor is he dissatisfied with it; he has simply never considered it, and never will.

But advocates of whole-life satisfactionism need not be embarrassed by this, for they can claim that whole-life satisfactionism was never meant to be a theory of episodic happiness. Just what the theory is supposed to be about may differ from theorist to theorist; for the purposes of our discussion, we will understand whole-life satisfactionism to be a theory just of *happiness in life*. Thus, it can agree with hedonism about episodic happiness; it just has to disagree with hedonism about happiness in life.

This fits with how some scientists of happiness see things. According to happiness pioneer Ed Diener and colleagues, for example, there are "two varieties of happiness": "a person's momentary feelings and thoughts about well-being, and larger, more global constructions" (Diener et al. 2002: 65). "At the momentary level [think episodic happiness] we can examine people's reports of moods, pleasures, pains, and satisfactions recorded online through the experience sampling method" (Diener et al. 2002: 65). Global constructions, by contrast, can be measured using something in the neighborhood of Diener's influential "Satisfaction with Life Scale," which asks subjects how strongly they agree with statements such as "I am satisfied with my life" and "In most ways my life is close to my ideal" (Diener et al. 2002: 70).

What about dispositional happiness? Because hedonists take happiness in life to be an aggregation of episodic happiness, there will, for hedonists, be little, if any, distinction in practice between being disposed to be episodically happy and being disposed to be happy in life. But because whole-life satisfactionists can hold that happiness in life is quite a different kind of thing from episodic happiness, it would be natural for whole-life satisfactionists to believe in two distinct kinds of dispositional happiness: dispositional episodic happiness and dispositional happiness in life.

Sumner is a whole-life satisfactionist about "*being happy/having a happy life*," which it is reasonable to understand as the same thing as our happiness in life. According to Sumner, happiness in this sense has two components: a cognitive component, consisting in "a positive evaluation of the conditions of your life, . . . a judgement that, on balance and taking everything into account, your life is going well for you"; and an affective component (i.e., one relating to feelings and emotions), which consists in feeling satisfied or fulfilled by your life (Summer 1996: 145, 146).

Elizabeth Telfer is another champion of the life-satisfaction theory. She identifies more or less our three main happiness notions: episodic happiness, happiness in life, and dispositional happiness. Interestingly, Telfer characterizes episodic happiness simply as: "'Happy' meaning 'enjoyable' or 'pleasant'" (Telfer 1980: 2). She thus appears to take it as obvious that there is a sense of happiness for which hedonism is correct. But Telfer is a whole-life satisfactionist about happiness in life. Her view is simpler than Sumner's, and even hedonically tinged: "My suggestion for a definition of happiness [in life]," she writes, "is that it is a state of being pleased with one's life as a whole" (Telfer 1980: 2). What makes Telfer's account of happiness in life crucially different from hedonism's is that, for hedonists, you are happy in life if you accumulate enough episodes within your life of being pleased about things (whatever things you like); but for Telfer, to be happy in life is to take up your life as an object of contemplation and to be pleased with it.

This shows that the crucial distinction between hedonism and whole-life satisfactionism doesn't so much concern the precise subjective attitudes involved in each view, but instead whether happiness in a life is determined by aggregating subjective states occurring throughout a life or by consulting the subjective states that one takes up toward one's whole life.

Still, there are differences among whole-life-satisfaction theories on the question of just which attitude toward one's life makes for happiness in life, and among the possible answers here, there is a certain distinction that merits mention. This is the distinction between (a) an attitude that actually manifests in the subject – the subject actually considers her life and takes up the attitude toward it – and (b) an attitude that is merely dispositional or hypothetical: the subject *would* take it up if certain conditions were met – for example, if the subject were to be asked to consider and evaluate her life as a whole. This distinction merits special mention because it can interact in interesting ways with dispositional notions of happiness, which we introduced earlier. For instance, if a whole-life-satisfaction theory employs dispositional attitudes, it may make sense for the theory to be put forth as a theory of a dispositional happiness concept, such as dispositional happiness in life, rather than as a theory of regular, non-dispositional happiness in life.

In addition to the question of which attitude toward one's life makes for happiness in life, whole-life-satisfaction theories differ also on the question of what the object of the attitude needs to be for happiness to occur. At one extreme is the view of Polish philosopher Władysław Tatarkiewicz, according to whom:

> Satisfaction with life as a whole must be satisfaction not only with that which is, but also with that which was and that which will be, not only with the present, but also with the past and the future. The feeling of happiness thus includes not only an agreeable present state, but also a favourable assessment of the past and good chance for the anticipated future. (Tatarkiewicz 1976: 140)

The view of Richard Brandt is at the other end of the spectrum and allows that having a positive attitude merely toward certain *aspects* of one's life contributes to happiness (Brandt 1967: 414); the more aspects of one's life that one likes, the happier one counts as being. To some extent then, Brandt's theory takes the "whole" out of whole-life satisfactionism and makes it more closely resemble the aggregative approach characteristic of hedonism. Perhaps it shouldn't even be categorized together with the other whole-life-satisfaction theories we've been considering.

Due to these important differences among whole-life-satisfaction theories, we'll formulate the theory schematically; and we'll understand it just as a theory about happiness in life, leaving whole-life satisfactionists free to endorse some other account of episodic happiness:

Whole-Life Satisfactionism about Happiness in Life:
(i) To be *happy* – that is, to have happiness in life – is to have a certain positive attitude or set of attitudes toward one's life as whole (or else just one's

whole *present* life); to be *unhappy* – that is, to have unhappiness in life – is to have a certain negative attitude or set of attitudes toward one's life as whole (or else just one's whole *present* life);

(ii) One's degree of happiness or unhappiness in life is a function of the strength of the relevant attitudes.

Compare this with hedonism's view of happiness in life. For hedonists, happiness in life is in a certain way "objective" and "bottom up" (I borrow these usages from Kahneman 1999). It is objective in that, on this view, it doesn't matter how the subject feels about their life; all that matters is the number and magnitude of episodes of happiness/pleasure and unhappiness/pain contained within it. A subject might, if asked, reject their life as a miserable waste of time, but if they are nevertheless regularly experiencing episodic happiness day-to-day – they are happy to be taking their morning walk, they are happy that their motorcycle is finally running well, etc. – and not so much episodic unhappiness, their life will count as a happy one whether they like it or not. To be sure, hedonists would not disregard their feeling that their own life is a miserable waste of time; for the displeasure involved in this assessment is yet another displeasure to include in the aggregation. But it would have no special status, and would detract from their happiness in life no more than equally intense displeasure taken in something more quotidian. Happiness in life is "bottom up" according to hedonism in that it is built up out of smaller, more basic ingredients: our moment-to-moment episodes of happiness/pleasure and unhappiness/pain.

Whole-life satisfactionism, by contrast, is more "subjectivist" and "top down." To determine how happy a person's life is, whole-life satisfactionism doesn't aggregate from the moments of their life but instead consults how they feel about the whole thing. Whereas on hedonism, if a person is happy in life, this is, as it were, *built into it*, on whole-life satisfactionism, it is *conferred on it*, by the subject's attitudes about it.

Hedonism, we saw, fits well with moment-based experience-sampling measures of happiness. Whole-life satisfactionism fits well with the other main category of happiness measurement: global instruments that ask participants to reflect on their lives as wholes and report on how well their lives measure up to their ideals, how satisfied or happy they are with their lives, how well their lives are going, and so forth.

3.3.1 Evaluating Whole-Life Satisfactionism

Which is the more plausible account of happiness in life: hedonism's more objective, aggregative, bottom-up conception or whole-life satisfactionism's more subjective, holistic, top-down conception? Here we are asking which of these conceptions better matches our pre-theoretical concept of happiness in life. When we make remarks such as:

> "OK, but are you *happy*?"
> "I had a happy childhood"
> "I didn't realize it until now, but I've been unhappy for some time"
> "You should choose the career that will make you happiest"

is the happiness concept that appears in them an aggregative, bottom-up concept or a holistic, top-down concept? When a person says that they had a happy childhood, are they saying something along the lines of that their childhood contained lots of experiences of episodic happiness and not so many of episodic unhappiness, or instead something in the ballpark of that if they were to reflect on their childhood as a whole, they would be satisfied with it or judge that it measures up?

This is not an easy question to answer. And perhaps it is even presenting a false dichotomy: maybe we sometimes have the aggregative, bottom-up notion in mind when we make such remarks and other times the holistic, top-down notion. If so, then we likely have two senses of happiness here rather than one: there is *aggregative, bottom-up happiness in life* and there is *holistic, top-down happiness in life*. If that is indeed the structure of our happiness concepts, then we should interpret hedonism as offering an account of the former notion and whole-life satisfactionism the latter. There would then be no genuine dispute between the two theories; they would be theories of different phenomena.

In addition to this reconciliatory option, which multiplies senses of happiness, there is a compromise option that retains a single concept, but requires each party to expand their theory. They would each expand it to a pluralist view according to which happiness in life is a function of *both* bottom-up aggregation and top-down assessment. To be sure, hedonism already can count as both; that's because it will count any top-down attitudes about one's life when the having of those attitudes is either pleasant or painful. So, to be a distinctive view, the pluralist view I am imagining would have to do one of two things. One is to *give special weight to the top-down attitudes*. If the relevant attitudes on this view are attitudes of being pleased about one's life (as on Telfer's non-pluralist view), then these pleasures would have to count for more toward one's happiness in life than equally strong pleasures taken in other things. Alternatively, the pluralist view could *make the top-down attitudes non-hedonic*, such as a bare judgment about how well one's life measures up to one's standards. Either way, the pluralist view would hold that the two categories of mental state – top-down assessments and bottom-up aggregations – both contribute to happiness in life so that it is possible to be happy in life with enough of just one of them, and that the more one gets of either, the happier one's life is. Interestingly, a recently popular way of measuring happiness reflects this pluralist view; this is a method that combines experience sampling with life-satisfaction surveys.

Where does this leave us on the dispute over the nature of happiness in life? One reaction is not to worry so much what the sample sentences above are really about, whether it's bottom-up aggregation, top-down assessment, sometimes one, sometimes the other, always both, or always in some way indeterminate between the two. We've got these two phenomena in any case, and the important issue is not so much which one is being referred to with which sentences of English, but which phenomenon is more worthy of our attention. Which is the phenomenon that is the better candidate for being a welfare good and the phenomenon that policymakers should be trying to promote in society?

In what follows, then, we'll consider two kinds of challenge: challenges to the idea that happiness in life amounts to whole-life satisfaction and challenges to the idea that whole-life satisfaction is importantly relevant to well-being.

Changing Assessments

Whole-life satisfactionism says, in a nutshell, that your life is a happy one if and only if you are satisfied with it. But the attitude that a person has toward one and the same thing can change over time. What if Ailsa is satisfied with her life as a whole today at noon, but tonight at midnight she will, for some reason, be dissatisfied with that very same life? Suppose we are wondering whether that life is a happy one. What is the answer to our question?

One natural reaction is to ask what caused Ailsa's change in evaluation. Maybe she learned something new about her life. This might motivate the whole-life satisfactionist to construct her theory in a way that favors the more informed assessment. But suppose Ailsa's change in evaluation is not due to a change in what she knows about her life. Perhaps it is due to a change in her standards of evaluation.

The whole-life satisfactionist may have no way of avoiding holding that *relative to noon* Ailsa's life is a happy life, *relative to midnight* it is an unhappy life, and that's that: there is no privileged perspective from which we can determine whether this life is "really" happy. This seems like an awkward result. It would also make it difficult for happiness researchers to know what to do. If they know all of these facts about Ailsa, should they put her down as one of the happy ones or one of the unhappy ones?

Bottom-up aggregative views like hedonism don't have this problem. The sum of a person's episodic happiness less her episodic unhappiness over some period of time is an unchanging quantity.

Absent Assessments

We sensibly talk and think about the happiness of young children and animals, and this includes wondering about their happiness in life. "I know your dog wasn't very happy when you were living right in town – he always seemed anxious," someone might remark, "but now that you are living in the mountains, is your dog happy?" This would seem to be a question about happiness in life. And it seems to be a reasonable question. But if a whole-life satisfaction theory is true (or at least a non-dispositionalized version [see below]), the matter is settled straightaway: no, your dog is not happy, because he lacks the ability to consider his life as a whole.

But that seems wrong. Some dogs do have happy lives. Moreover, it seems fairly plausible that what determines whether a dog has a happy life is simply the number and strength of their states of episodic happiness and unhappiness. Perhaps, then, the same is true for people.

In response to this objection, a whole-life satisfactionist might resort to a bifurcated approach, holding that their view of happiness in life is true only for adult humans, the bottom-up aggregative view being the true theory for animals and young children. The pluralist option mentioned above would also be worth considering here: if your dog has lots of episodes of happiness and not many episodes of unhappiness, he'll count as happy in life on the pluralist view – and he might have counted as even happier if he had had the capacity to assess his own life.

But problems of absent attitudes don't end with animals and children. Normal adults can lack such attitudes, too. It is possible for a person to live ever in the moment, always engaged with whatever they are doing at the time, never giving any thought to their life as a whole, much less making an assessment of it. Whole-life-satisfaction theories that appeal to actual life satisfaction (as opposed to hypothetical or dispositional life satisfaction) would be forced to say that such a person is not happy. But, just as with your dog, if the person's life were rich with episodes of happiness and they were rarely episodically unhappy, we would think of them as having happy lives, despite their lack of whole-life satisfaction.

A natural way for the whole-life satisfactionist to try to deal with this is to dispositionalize their theory, and hold that happiness in life is determined by the attitudes that (on one version) one *would* have if one *were* to consider one's life as a whole. But these dispositional views (along with the kind of view we've been discussing, the view that appeals to actual life satisfaction) face a problem of mismatch, to which we now turn.

Mismatched Assessments

An attraction of whole-life satisfactionism is that it is supposed to make the subject themself a kind of author of their own happiness. They get to say whether they are happy, via the assessments they make of, or satisfactions they take in, their own life. Others' attitudes toward the subject's life have no such power, nor even do they subject's own day-to-day experiences get to settle the matter, as hedonists hold. Only the subject themself gets to.

But this authority can look implausible when the assessment a person makes of their life fails to fit its contents. Nothing bars a person who is usually episodically happy and rarely episodically unhappy from forming a dim view of their own life and being wholly dissatisfied with it. Is such a person *happy*? Whole-life satisfactionists must say no. This may strike you as the wrong result; their life is full of happiness after all.

The reverse is also possible. A person with a busy, high-powered career might be satisfied with their life and judge it to meet or exceed their ideals, yet day-to-day they are always some combination of anxious, annoyed, and exhausted. That their life is long on suffering and short on enjoyment strongly suggests that, however they judge their life, they are simply not happy. But whole-life satisfactionists must say otherwise.

Problems of mismatch affect dispositionalized whole-life satisfaction theories too. One way to dispositionalize a whole-life satisfaction theory is to have it appeal to the attitudes one would have if one were fully informed about one's life and thinking clearly about it. But even someone fully informed about their life and thinking clearly about it can make an assessment of it that is at odds with its contents.

Mismatched assessments make less if any trouble for the pluralist option we have been considering. This view puts independent weight on the contents irrespective of the top-down assessment. However, note that, relatedly, this view does not deliver the idea that each of us is an authority on our own happiness in the sense characterized above.

These last two objections – absence and mismatch – are an occasion to reflect on which phenomenon – bottom-up aggregation or top-down assessment – is more important. When we are deciding how *good* someone's life was for them, is it more important to consider the content of that life or how the person would have assessed that content? Suppose you are a policymaker charged with picking between two policies. One will change people's lives in a way that improves their day-to-day experiences without making them judge their lives any better; the other will change people's lives in ways that make them rate their lives more favorably, but without improving their day-to-day experiences. Which policy should we prefer? One way to begin trying to answer this question – essentially a question about well-being – is to ask yourself which option you would prefer for yourself, and which option you think would give you a better life.

Problems of Bias and Lability

The final problem that we'll catalog for whole-life satisfactionism (although it may be less of a problem for some dispositionalized theories) comes from empirical research on the factors that affect judgments about our lives. It turns out that these judgments can be biased in systematic ways, and can be affected by factors that even the judger would admit should be irrelevant.

Colonoscopies used to be performed without sedation and could be very painful. The level of pain would vary during the procedure, from none at all to almost unbearable. Psychologists have wanted to know how well people gauge the quality of their recent experiences, so they have studied colonoscopies. Researchers first ask subjects undergoing colonoscopies to rate their pain in real time (think bottom-up experience sampling). Then, after the procedure ends, they ask these same subjects to rate how bad the ordeal was as a whole (think top-down assessment). What they found was striking. Subjects' top-down assessments of how painful the ordeal was do not match how painful it actually was, as determined by aggregating the moment-by-moment data. Instead, subjects conform to the "peak-end rule": their assessments are very heavily influenced by how bad the ordeal's worst moment was (its peak) and how bad its ending was. Astonishingly, *duration* of procedure – which I take it we all agree matters a great deal – "had no effect whatsoever on the ratings of total pain" (Kahneman 2011: 380). Psychologist Daniel Kahneman, one champion of these studies, concludes that our top-down assessments are worth little, and it is our moment-to-moment experiences that matter.

These studies were about assessing a medical procedure in terms of how painful it is rather than a life in terms of how good or satisfying it is, but studies by Ed Diener and colleagues have shown that the peak-end rule and duration neglect also govern our assessments of entire lives (Kahneman 2011: 387).

A related problem is that when subjects are asked to make assessments of their lives as wholes, they base these judgments on only a partial consideration of the object of their evaluation – which is understandable, given the difficulty of considering one's whole life. Information about one's life that one has considered *recently* – for instance, in connection with a previous question in the questionnaire being used to assess whole-life satisfaction – tends to play an outsize role in shaping how one feels about one's whole life (Schwarz and Strack 1999).

Another problem is that even if we manage to consider our whole lives, the standards by which we evaluate them can be influenced by contextual factors in a way that seems to rob the judgments of their authority. For example, if a person with a visible disability is present while a subject is reporting on his life satisfaction, he will likely rate his life more highly than he would if the person with the disability were not present (Schwarz and Strack 1999: 77).

Yet another problem is that the mood one happens to be in at the time one is considering one's life can significantly affect what one thinks of it. This is especially troubling given how fickle our moods can be. According to research by German psychologist Norbert Schwarz:

> Finding a dime on a copy machine (Schwarz 1987), spending time in a pleasant rather than an unpleasant room (Schwarz et al. 1987, Experiment 2), or watching the German soccer team win rather than lose a championship game (Schwarz et al. 1987, Experiment 1) all resulted in increased reports of happiness and satisfaction with one's life as a whole. (Schwarz and Strack 1999)

But one's assessment of one's life is supposed to be a response to the contents of that life. If it can be manipulated so easily, it is hard to think that we should infer much about how happy that life really is from this assessment. It's even harder to think that these assessments should determine a person's well-being or influence policymakers.

The fickleness of our feelings about our lives does not make similar trouble for bottom-up conceptions of happiness in life. The reason is that when our mood rises for some trivial reason (we found a dime), it is not implausible to hold that this pleasant mood contributes a tiny bit to our happiness, which is all that hedonists would be committed to saying. But whole-life satisfactionists must say that that one little dime has the power to endow one's whole life with a good bit more happiness.

This concludes our discussion of the two most prominent theories of the nature of happiness, hedonism and whole-life satisfactionism, the exemplars of the two main ways of determining happiness in life (bottom-up or top-down). In the remainder of this section, we'll discuss much more briefly three additional theories.

3.4 The Emotional-State Theory of Happiness

The emotional-state theory of happiness is new on the scene, at least when treated as a theory distinct from hedonism, and is most associated with philosopher Daniel Haybron. Its essence is the identification of happiness with an overall positive emotional condition. It is similar to hedonism, and is sometimes lumped in with it, but its advocates stress its differences, typically claiming that not all pleasures constitute states of happiness and not all happiness-constituting states are pleasures.

What concept of happiness are emotional-state theories theories of? Haybron says that his is a theory of "happiness in the long-term psychological sense," which, he emphasizes: "[S]hould be distinguished from the acute emotion or mood of *feeling* happy" (Haybron 2008: 32, 30). I interpret Haybron as having episodic happiness in mind with the latter, and, with the former, either happiness in life, dispositional happiness, or both. I include dispositional happiness here because Haybron's theory makes heavy use of dispositional mental states in explaining happiness. Other advocates of the emotional-state approach (Kauppinen 2013, Rossi 2018) depart from Haybron's focus on dispositional states and, as I interpret them, intend their theory to account for episodic happiness and happiness in life. For the sake of simplicity and brevity, I will formulate the emotional-state theory in this non-dispositional way:

The Emotional-State Theory of Happiness:

  (i) To experience episodic happiness is to experience positive emotion, such as joy or relief; to experience episodic unhappiness is to experience negative emotion, such as sadness or irritation;

  (ii) To be *happy* – that is, to have happiness in life – is for one's overall emotional condition to be positive; to be *unhappy* is for one's overall emotional condition to be negative.

  (iii) Dispositional happiness (or unhappiness) consists in certain positive (or negative) dispositional states, such as unconscious emotions and moods of a positive (or negative) sort, and in propensities to experience positive (or negative) emotions and moods.

One popular way of measuring happiness fits well with the emotional-state theory. This is the Positive and Negative Affect Schedule (PANAS), a questionnaire that measures just what you'd guess: positive affect or emotion (e.g., excitedness, enthusiasm, pride) and negative affect or emotion (e.g., irritability, distress, fear).

Recall the strongest objection to hedonism about happiness, that on hedonism: "[A]ll sorts of shallow, fleeting pleasures are made to count toward happiness" (Haybron 2008: 63). Emotional-state theories can avoid this problem. When you bite into a cracker and experience a pleasant taste, this often has no impact on your emotional state. And that is why it often has no impact on your happiness, according to the emotional-state theory.[6]

One crucial question for the emotional-state theory is: What makes an emotion a *positive* emotion? One possible answer is hedonic: it is for the emotion to be pleasant. Does combining the emotional-state theory of happiness with this hedonic view of emotion's valence collapse the emotional-state theory into hedonism? Not necessarily. For perhaps there are some pleasant experiences – the taste of the cracker is a plausible candidate – that involve no emotion. Hedonism about happiness would say that such cases still involve happiness (because they involve pleasure), while an emotional-state theory would maintain that they don't involve happiness (because they don't involve emotion). An emotional-state theory that appeals to the hedonic view of emotion's valence would be saying that happiness requires a state that is both an emotion *and* pleasant.

One final clarification about the emotional-state theory: some advocates offer complex accounts of which features of an emotion determine how much that emotion contributes to happiness. It may not be just a matter of the intensity and duration of the positive emotion; also important may be its connections to other mental states and to behavior, the extent to which the emotion permeates the whole of consciousness, and how deep or profound the emotion feels.

We will close this subsection with two brief possible objections to the emotional-state approach. One is that not all positive emotions are clearly happiness-constituting – for example, admiration (Kauppinen 2013: 173). If that's right, then the core idea of the theory will require revision; only certain positive emotions will contribute to happiness, and advocates of this approach will need to say which ones, and why.

Another possible problem is that perhaps not all happiness-constituting states are emotional. Imagine someone waiting on a subway platform for their train to arrive. They are in an emotionally neutral state of mind, although they would like the train to show up soon. And then it does. They look down the tracks and see it coming, and are happy that it is coming. Must they therefore be experiencing emotion at that time? Although I admit that the answer is not obvious, perhaps this is a case of emotionless happiness. If so, this would seem to strike at the very heart of the emotional-state approach.

---

[6] Haybron's own explanation of why such cases don't involve happiness relies more heavily on his view that happiness "primarily concerns ... dispositions" (Haybron 2008: 69). Mauro Rossi, another emotional-state theorist, argues that sensory pleasures of the sort that saltine crackers cause *do* constitute states of happiness (Rossi 2018).

3.5 Desire-Satisfaction Theories of Happiness

Another approach to happiness goes farther back in history than the emotional-state theory but gets less attention than the hedonistic tradition. This is the desire-satisfaction approach to happiness. The great German philosopher Immanuel Kant held that:

> *Happiness* is the condition of a rational being in the world with whom *everything goes according to his wish and his will.* (Kant 1788: 150)

According to philosopher V. J. McGill:

> the root meaning of "happiness" appears to be something like this: A lasting state of affairs in which the most favorable ratio of satisfied desires to desires is realized, with the proviso that the satisfied desires can include satisfactions that are not preceded by specific desires for them, but come by surprise. (McGill 1967: 5)

Wayne Davis's theory of happiness is also desire-based, but in an importantly different way:

> Take every proposition [that some subject] A is thinking at the moment, multiply the degree to which it is believed by the degree to which it is desired, add up all the products, and the sum is A's degree of happiness. (Davis 1981a: 113)

My own view is that Davis's approach is very much on the right track as an account of episodic happiness, with happiness in life and dispositional happiness being explained in terms of episodic happiness, in the way hedonists do. I'll say more about this in the final section of the Element.

3.6 Eudaimonism about Happiness

The final theory of happiness that we'll look at is eudaimonism about happiness, whose name derives from the Greek adjective *eudaimon*. Its etymological meaning is *favored by the gods*, but in the works of Aristotle, the notion's foremost champion, "eudaimon" is usually translated as "happy," "flourishing," or "successful."

I have thus far been assuming that we can figure out the true theory of happiness independently of our attempts to figure out the true theory of well-being. I was assuming that the former endeavor is value-neutral while the latter is value-laden. But some views of the nature of happiness have it that these questions are more deeply entangled, that happiness is itself an evaluative phenomenon, not a purely descriptive, psychological one.

For example, philosopher Julia Annas writes: "As we bring up our children, what we aim for is not that they have episodes of smiley-face feeling" –

here she has in mind episodic happiness – "but that their lives go well as wholes: we come to think of happiness as the way a life as a whole goes well" (Annas 2004: 45). Annas is suggesting that when we claim that someone has a happy life, we are not describing their psychology; we are evaluating their life.

Annas admits that we do use the term "happiness" to talk about "episodes of smiley-face feeling," that is, episodic happiness. She also admits that many people prefer terms such as "flourishing or welfare or well-being rather than happiness" to talk about what she is using "happiness" to talk about. "These terms may be useful in some circumstances to avoid misunderstanding," she acknowledges, "but we should not yield talk of happiness without further discussion to its most trivial contexts of use" (Annas 2004: 45).

I understand Annas to be suggesting that perhaps the concept of *episodic happiness* is merely descriptive, and its content is in the ballpark of what the hedonists or desire satisfactionists about episodic happiness say it is, but the concept of *happiness in life* is crucially different, and is, in fact, evaluative.

Those who identify with the eudaimonist tradition tend to hold not just that happiness in life is an evaluative notion – and in particular the notion of well-being – they also tend to endorse a certain specific account of well-being: a perfectionist one. This makes sense. It would be odd to argue that happiness in life amounts to well-being and is not just a matter of smiley-face feelings while at the same time being willing to accept a smiley-face-feeling (hedonist) account of well-being. Here, then, is our formulation of

Eudaimonism about Happiness:
  (i)   To be *happy* – that is, to have happiness in life – is to be well-off;
  (ii) To be *unhappy* – that is, to have unhappiness in life – is to be badly off;
  (iii) Being well or badly off is explained by perfectionism about well-being: a being is well-off to the extent that its nature is developed, realized, or exercised.

Writers who aim to elucidate the nature of happiness in life tend to assume that even if this concept has an evaluative reading on which it means well-being, it also has a descriptive, psychological reading. And they simply set aside the evaluative reading, stipulating the psychological one to be the target of their investigation. Eudaimonists about happiness challenge this very setup. They hold that when I ask in my example, "OK, but are you *happy*?", I am asking a certain thing, and that thing is not a question in psychology. It a question that is fundamentally about value.

* * * * *

This concludes our discussion of the nature of happiness. Certainly no consensus has been reached on this issue by the philosophers who work on it, and this matters for the theory of well-being, inasmuch as it is hard to be confident whether happiness is among the basic welfare goods while being unsure what happiness even is. In the next section, I sketch the theory of the nature of happiness that I find plausible and explain how it fits into a subjective theory of well-being, but the issue of the nature of happiness continues to attract the attention of researchers as much as the theory of well-being.

4 Varieties of Subjectivism about Well-Being

We clarified the topic of well-being in Section 1. We explored the distinction between objective and subjective accounts of well-being in Section 2. This included examining the main advantages and disadvantages of each and some challenges specific to the two main varieties of objective theory. Section 3 was about happiness rather than well-being and examined in depth the two most important theories of happiness, hedonism and whole-life satisfactionism, before briefly discussing some other important theories. In this final section, we dive more deeply into subjective theories of well-being, the approach to well-being that I find more promising.

4.1 Hedonism about Well-Being

Hedonism about well-being is one of the oldest philosophical doctrines still discussed and defended today. It claims that *all* the episodes of pleasure that we experience make our lives better for us (this is somewhat controversial) and that *only* these do that (this is much more controversial). More fully, we have:

Hedonism about Well-Being:
  (i) Every episode of pleasure is basically good for the subject experiencing it; every episode of pain is basically bad for the subject experiencing it; nothing else is basically good or bad for anyone.
 (ii) The basic prudential value of a pleasure or pain is determined by its magnitude, which is a function of its intensity and duration.
(iii) The prudential value of a life or life-segment in itself = the sum of the basic prudential values of all of the pleasures and pains that occur within it.

Outside philosophy, a "hedonist" is a seeker of physical pleasure (that of food, intoxication, sex, etc.). But the philosophical doctrine of hedonism does not imply that this should be our priority. For one thing, hedonism is not the sociopathic view that only one's own pleasure and pain matter. For another, it is far from clear that the way to maximize the balance of pleasure over pain in one's life is to pursue bodily pleasures. The pleasures of sex, drugs, and rock 'n' roll can bring disease, heartbreak, addiction, and tinnitus. For as long as the view has been advocated, hedonists have emphasized the greater reliability, durability, and freedom from painful side-effects of the pleasures of the mind.

Is hedonism an objective or a subjective theory of well-being? Interestingly, it depends on what pleasure is, an issue that also affects the plausibility of hedonism.

4.1.1 The Nature of Pleasure

There are at least these two importantly different kinds of mental state: *sensations* and *propositional attitudes*. Sensations include the feeling of touching velvet, the smell sensation of coffee brewing, and nausea. Propositional attitudes include beliefs, desires, hopes, fears: states of mind that have a proposition – something that can be true or false – as its object. Consider the proposition that it is right now raining outside where you are. You can believe this, you can desire this, you can fear this, you can doubt this. Our propositional attitudes can also be about our own sensations, as when a person wants to be smelling the freshly brewing coffee that they are smelling.

Two kinds of pleasure correspond to the two kinds of mental state above. There is *sensory pleasure*, which many of us experience when we bite into a juicy peach or feel the bodily sensations of stepping into a warm bath on a cold day. And there is *attitudinal pleasure*, which is more intellectual; it is what one experiences when one is pleased that or takes pleasure in the fact that something is the case. For example, when Tiger Woods won the Masters in 2019, I took pleasure in that fact.

Theories of the nature of pleasure aim to tell us what pleasure of both sorts is. On one way of seeing things, they divide into two main kinds: *sensation-based theories* and *attitude-based theories*. Sensation-based theories explain all pleasure, whether sensory or attitudinal, in terms of sensations, and attitude-based theories in terms of attitudes. Note that the sensation/attitude distinction has now appeared three times: for mental states in general, for pleasure in particular, and now for *theories* of pleasure. It arises for unpleasant states too, but we'll focus on the positive.

The Distinctive-Feeling Theory of Pleasure

One kind of sensation-based theory is the *distinctive-feeling theory*. On this view, pleasure is simply its own kind of sensation. Alongside the sensations of seeing cobalt blue, of smelling a rose, and of "pins and needles" in the foot, there is the sensation of pleasure. The nature of this sensation is in an important sense ineffable on this view, but that is no objection, since the same is true of all basic sensations. Here is John Locke, the great seventeenth-century British philosopher:

> Amongst the simple ideas, which we receive both from sensation and reflection, pain and pleasure are two very considerable ones ... These, like other simple ideas, cannot be described, nor their names defined; the way of knowing them is, as of the simple ideas of the senses, only by experience. (Locke 1689: II, xx, 1; see also Moore 1903: §12 and Bramble 2013)

On the distinctive-feeling theory, sensory pleasure occurs when a sensory experience (e.g., the smell of a lilac bush) causes another sensory experience, the feeling of pleasure itself. Attitudinal pleasure occurs when attending to or noticing some fact (e.g., that Tiger Woods has won the Masters) causes one to experience the sensation of pleasure.

One challenge to this view is the *heterogeneity problem*. The distinctive-feeling theory implies that there is a specific sensory experience common to all cases in which we experience pleasure, in the same way that there is a specific sensory experience common to cases in which we, say, look at a traffic cone (the experience of that particular shade of orange). But pleasure does not seem to be so homogenous. Consider the pleasure involved in each of the following: seeing that one is getting some writing in, figuring out a crossword clue that one has been stuck on, biting into a cold plum on a hot day, and getting a foot massage. There seems to be no one sensation common to all four cases.

Another challenge is the *isolation problem*. The distinctive-feeling theory predicts, contrary to what we seem to find, that it should be possible to experience the sensation of pleasure in isolation from all other sensations and thoughts. We should be able to experience *only pleasure*, alongside nothing else. For this is how it is with sensations in general. We could float you in an isolation tank and get you into a state in which you are experiencing no sensations. We could then expose you to a certain smell – of basil, say. You could then be experiencing the smell of basil and nothing else. But the analogous thing does not seem conceivable with pleasure, contrary to what the distinctive-feeling theory implies.

The Hedonic-Tone Theory of Pleasure

Maybe the problem with the distinctive-feeling theory isn't that it makes pleasure a sensory thing, but it makes it *too specific* a sensory thing. Maybe pleasure is more abstract: a *way* that other sensations can be, or a dimension along which sensations vary. This is the claim of the hedonic-tone theory, first advocated in 1930 by the philosopher C. D. Broad. On this theory, all experiences fall somewhere on a hedono-doloric spectrum, ranging from *very pleasurable* to *neutral* to *very unpleasant*. Sensations from a massage have the very pleasurable hedonic tone, as does the experience of receiving a standing ovation. Many experiences – the hum of my refrigerator – are hedonically neutral. The pinprick sensation from a flu shot has a mild doloric tone.

How does the hedonic-tone theory accommodate the fact that it is not possible to experience pleasure in perfect isolation? An interesting analogy due to philosopher Shelly Kagan illustrates how (Kagan 1992: 127). Consider *loudness*, which is a feature of certain sound sensations. It is not possible to experience loudness in perfect isolation: there always has to be some sound sensation (the sound of a high B♭ on a trumpet, the sound of a jackhammer) that has the loudness. If pleasure is like this, as the hedonic-tone theory can hold, we have an explanation of why it is not possible to experience pleasure in perfect isolation.

Does the hedonic-tone theory also solve the heterogeneity problem? Consider again the pleasures involved in seeing that I am getting some writing in, figuring out a crossword clue, and getting a foot massage. Although it's hard to say, maybe they do have in common a single more abstract thing, a hedonic tone, in the way that the sound of a high B♭ played loudly on a trumpet and the sound of a jackhammer have in common *loudness*.

But here is a different problem for the theory. Loudness of sensation is a feature of sensations that is determined by the intrinsic quality of the sensation. Sensations that are duplicates as regards their intrinsic qualities must be duplicates as regards their loudness. But this does not seem to be the case for pleasure. Two sensations that are intrinsically exactly alike can differ in how pleasurable they are. Consider the taste of olives. In me, that taste is unpleasant, but this same taste sensation in Shankar is pleasurable. Yet the gustatory qualities of the taste sensations in Shankar and me may for all this be identical. A hedonic-tone theory modelled on the loudness analogy thus cannot accommodate what we might call the *independent variability* of pleasure: the fact that duplicate sensations can differ hedonically.

Interestingly, the distinctive-feeling theory has no problem here. On this view, the taste of olives is unpleasant in me but pleasant in Shankar because it causes the sensation of unpleasantness in me but the sensation of pleasure in Shankar.

The hedonic-tone theory could abandon the analogy with loudness and hold that the connection between a sensation's non-hedonic and hedonic qualities is causal and merely contingent rather than necessary (see Broad 1930: 231). But this threatens to turn the hedonic-tone theory back into the distinctive-feeling theory.

Attitude-Based Theories of Sensory Pleasure

Is there a theory can solve all three problems: heterogeneity, isolation, and independent variability? Yes. Broad himself mentions it:

> Is it not possible that what we have called "hedonic *quality*" is really a *relational property* and not a quality at all? Is it not possible that the statement: "This experience of mine is pleasant" just means: "I like this experience for its non-hedonic qualities"? (Broad 1930: 237)

Broad is here describing an attitude-based approach to pleasure, to be contrasted with the two sensation-based approaches above.

In illustrating how attitude-based theories can accommodate our three phenomena, we'll begin by confining ourselves to sensory pleasure. Attitude-based views, such as the liking-based theory mentioned by Broad, accommodate the heterogeneity of sensory pleasure. What makes each of the sensations involved in biting into a cold plum, getting a foot massage, and smelling a lilac bush *pleasant* is not any further sensation it causes but the fact that the person experiencing it likes it. Another variety of attitude-based theory of pleasure is desire-based: what makes each pleasant is the fact that the person experiencing it has a desire to be experiencing it as they are experiencing it (Heathwood 2007). Yet another variety appeals to some cognitive state, such the sensation's seeming good (cf. Sidgwick 1907: 127).

Attitude-based theories also accommodate the finding that it is not possible to experience pleasure in isolation from other sensations and thoughts. On attitude-based theories, whenever we experience sensory pleasure, some sensation with non-hedonic qualities (e.g., the taste of the plum) must be present. This is because the theory holds that sensory pleasure occurs only when some sensation is the object of some positive attitude.

Attitude-based theories also accommodate the fact that duplicate sensations can differ hedonically. When Shankar enjoys an olive, he can, on this view, be getting exactly the same sensation I get, even though mine is unpleasant. What differs is the attitude being taken up toward the olive taste.

Attitude-Based Theories of Attitudinal Pleasure

Attitude-based theories of sensory pleasure thus seem promising. What about attitudinal pleasure? Recall that attitudinal pleasure, whatever it is, occurs when someone takes pleasure in something's being the case, or is pleased that something is the case. Right now I am pleased that I am getting some writing in, that my dog is lying next to me, and that it is sunny outside. The distinctive-feeling theory of pleasure would say that what it is for me to be pleased that I am getting some writing in is for the thought that I am getting some writing in to cause me to experience the sensation of pleasure. The hedonic-tone theory would say that it is for this thought to be hedonically toned. Attitude-based theories have two options: a non-reductionist and a reductionist option.

In general, to be a non-reductionist about some phenomenon is to hold that it cannot be identified with or otherwise explained in terms of some other phenomenon. A non-reductionist attitude-based account of attitudinal pleasure holds that attitudinal pleasure cannot be defined. This is the route taken by philosopher Fred Feldman, the foremost champion of the notion of attitudinal pleasure. His theories of both well-being (Feldman 2004) and happiness (Feldman 2010) are centered around it. Feldman writes:

> I am doubtful about the prospects for defining attitudinal pleasure, and so I propose to take it as my starting point. I will not offer an analysis of attitudinal pleasure, but will try to explain it in other ways. (Feldman 2010: 110)

This is one approach to attitudinal pleasure, but I favor a reductionist approach, which is more satisfying, if it can be made to work. On my view, attitudinal pleasure can be reduced to desire and belief: to be pleased that something is the case is to want it to be the case while simultaneously believing it to be the case. I am pleased right now that my dog is lying next to me. It's also true of me – as Feldman or anyone should agree – that I am aware that he is lying next to me and that I want him to be lying next to me. On my account, this is no coincidence: the latter pair of facts about belief and desire constitutes, explains, and reveals the nature of the former fact about attitudinal pleasure.

4.1.2 How the Nature of Pleasure Affects Its Value

In my view, attitude-based approaches to pleasure, in addition to being more plausible as theories of pleasure, have this further advantage: they alone vindicate the thought that pleasure is good in itself for those experiencing it. This is because only they enable the claim that pleasure is good in itself to conform to the resonance constraint. Recall that doctrine:

Resonance Constraint: A thing, x, is basically good for some subject, S, only if *either* S has a satisfied positive attitude toward x *or* x itself involves S's having a satisfied positive attitude toward something.

If an attitude-based theory of sensory pleasure is true, then the claim *that sensory pleasure is basically good for the subject experiencing it* conforms to the resonance constraint. Just how it does depends on the recondite question of precisely *which entity* the attitude-based theory says is the sensory pleasure. There are two options. The theory can say that the sensory pleasure is the *sensation* that is the object of the attitude (e.g., the taste sensation of the plum). Or it can say that it is the *combination* of the sensation and the attitude (which we might refer to using expressions such as "Carlos's liking the taste sensations he is getting from the plum"). On the former view, the claim *that these sensations (the pleasures) are intrinsically good* satisfies the resonance constraint because the subject of them would be having a satisfied positive attitude toward them. On the latter view, the claim *that the combination states (the pleasures) are intrinsically good* satisfies the resonance constraint because these states are themselves states of the subject's having a satisfied positive attitude toward something.

Similarly, both desire-based and non-reductionist theories of attitudinal pleasure enable the claim *that attitudinal pleasure is good in itself for the subject experiencing it* to conform to the resonance constraint. On the desire-based theory of attitudinal pleasure, this claim satisfies the resonance constraint because attitudinal pleasure states are states involving the subject's having a satisfied positive attitude (desire) toward something. And the same is true for attitudinal pleasure on the non-reductionist option, since attitudinal pleasure is itself a positive attitude, and one that is "automatically satisfied" (in the sense explained in 2.3.1 above). Both theories close off the possibility of being left cold while experiencing attitudinal pleasure.

This is in profound contrast to sensation-based theories of pleasure. Because on neither the distinctive-feeling theory nor the hedonic-tone theory is pleasure essentially attitude-involving, it is possible on these views to be left completely cold by pleasure. Consequently, neither theory allows the claim that pleasure is a basic welfare good to conform to the resonance constraint. Take the distinctive-feeling theory. Just as it is possible for someone to be indifferent to or averse to the taste of olives, it is possible for someone to be indifferent to or averse to pleasure itself – given this theory's conception of pleasure. Both sensation-based theories make hedonism an objective theory of well-being.

Because it is so plausible that at least innocent (non-malicious, etc.) pleasure is prudentially good and because it is at least rather plausible that whatever is prudentially good for us must be essentially pro-attitude-involving, this is evidence against these accounts of pleasure. And it should in any case make them less attractive to hedonists about well-being than their attitude-based competitors.

Just as sensation-based accounts of pleasure are unfriendly to hedonism, so too are reductionist accounts of attitudinal pleasure, though in a rather different way. Desire-based accounts of attitudinal pleasure hold that attitudinal pleasure is, at bottom, a species of desire satisfaction. If so, then an ostensibly hedonist theory of well-being that makes use of such a theory of pleasure isn't, at bottom, a hedonist theory after all; it is most fundamentally a desire-based theory.

Our conclusion, then, about how pleasure's nature bears on its value and on the defensibility of hedonism is this. Because attitude-based theories of the nature of pleasure make it more plausible that pleasure is good in itself, if you want to be a hedonist about well-being, it's best to reject sensation-based theories of pleasure in favor of attitude-based theories, which is justified on independent grounds anyway. Furthermore, if you want to be a hedonist, you should reject reductionism about attitudinal pleasure in favor of non-reductionism. Although he does not to my knowledge make this argument in favor of his view, I am here arguing in effect that if you want to be a hedonist, you should endorse Feldman's attitudinal hedonism. Only this view makes hedonism a subjectivist theory while avoiding collapse into another kind of subjectivist theory.

4.1.3 Arguments for Hedonism about Well-Being

We now take a look at a few arguments for hedonism about well-being.

From Psychological Hedonism

Although it is rarely taken seriously nowadays, we need to mention the most historically popular argument for hedonism about well-being: the argument from psychological hedonism. Psychological hedonism is a doctrine not about value but about what human beings desire:

Psychological Hedonism: The only thing that anyone wants for its own sake is their own pleasure and the only thing that anyone is averse to in itself is their own pain.

Accordingly, psychological hedonists hold that all human behavior is explained by the desire for pleasure and/or the aversion to pain. (We now have three importantly different doctrines labeled "hedonism": hedonism about happiness, hedonism about well-being, and psychological hedonism – not to mention the hedonic theory of positivity of emotion that we discussed briefly.) From psychological hedonism some draw the evaluative conclusion that the only thing that is good (or bad) in itself for a person is their own pleasure (or pain) – in other words, the core of hedonism is about well-being.

One serious problem with this argument is the dubiousness of psychological hedonism. I have preferences concerning what happens after my death. For example, I want the human species to continue. But I don't believe in an afterlife, so this desire cannot be explained by desires concerning how in my view the continuation of the human species after my death would affect my own pleasure or pain.

An even more serious problem for the argument from psychological hedonism for hedonism about well-being is that it undercuts itself. Even if we grant psychological hedonism, hedonism about well-being doesn't follow straightaway. It follows only with the help of a suppressed premise, a premise to the effect that only what a person desires for its own sake is good in itself for that person. But this suppressed premise conflicts with hedonism about well-being, the very doctrine the argument was meant to establish. It is the core of a competing theory of well-being, the desire-satisfaction theory.

From the Experience Requirement

Everyone knows the adage "what you don't know can't hurt you." There is something quite intuitive about it. An event occurs, you are not aware of it, you never will become aware of it, and it won't bring about any other events of which you will ever be aware. It thus never impinges in any way, directly or indirectly, on you or on your experience of the world. Your experiences and your whole picture of reality would have been exactly the same throughout your entire life had the event not occurred. Could such an event nevertheless be a benefit or a harm to you? The negative answer is pretty intuitive here.

Philosophers call this 'the experience requirement' on well-being. It says that a thing can be good for you only if it affects your experience in some way. Interestingly, this doctrine may be a kind of corollary of the resonance constraint, at least on some ways of interpreting the resonance constraint. The latter says that something must resonate with you if it is to benefit you. If something never affects your experience in any way, it could be argued that it would be right to say that it doesn't resonate with you.

The view that a thing can be good for you only if it affects your experience suggests that the only things that are of basic prudential value are experiences. Hedonism agrees. Thus, the experience requirement supports hedonism.

From Erroneous Intuitions

Probably the most common hedonist defense is a good offense: an attack of anti-hedonist intuitions. One kind of attack claims that it is a common mistake to attribute basic value to highly reliable derivative goods. If people invariably get pleasure from, say, finding out interesting things, this, the argument goes, can cause us to have the mistaken intuition that finding things out is good *in itself* for people, as an objective-list theory might hold, rather than good merely instrumentally. Other hedonists claim that there are advantages, for example evolutionarily, to having a tendency to believe that things other than pleasure have intrinsic value (Crisp 2006: 637–9). If an organism believes that mere survival is of basic prudential value, it may be more likely to survive than if it believes, what hedonism says is true, that survival is of mere instrumental value. If these sorts of empirical claims are true – something for which hedonists would need to provide evidence – we should be less confident in some anti-hedonist intuitions.

4.1.4 Objections to Hedonism about Well-Being

Resonance-constraint-based objections to hedonism target hedonisms that make use of sensation-based accounts of pleasure, but the most well-known objections to hedonism don't depend on what pleasure is.

Malicious Pleasure

One category of objection questions the claim that *all* pleasures are basically good for their subjects, even if many are. The classic counterexample is *malicious pleasure*, which we have already seen in the case of Ted Bundy. But there are less extreme cases, for example that of a boy who has fun throwing rocks at a duck (Kraut 1994). We also saw how subjectivists might respond to such objections. They, and hedonists too, can maintain that their theories do justice to the vague intuition that something is amiss with such pleasures (e.g., they are criticizable morally if not prudentially) and that that is enough.

Base Pleasure

A similar counterexample is that of *base pleasure*, such as that received from shooting heroin or having sex with animals (Moore 1903: §56). The kind of reply given to the objection from malicious pleasures might be less powerful here, because it's less obvious that such acts are morally wrong. But the more one doubts the moral objectionability of drug use or bestiality, the more one will doubt, I suspect, the original intuition that such pleasures are worthless.

But the objection from base pleasures can take a more moderate form. The key premise can claim not that base pleasures are worthless, but that they are worth less. A high from shooting heroin may feel good, and that's worth something, but the pleasures of communing with friends, appreciating beautiful works of art, and helping a stranger in need are worth more, even no greater in magnitude. In defiance of this intuition, hedonist Jeremy Bentham famously writes: "Prejudice apart, the game of push-pin [a children's game] is of equal value with the arts and sciences of music and poetry," prompting critics to describe the theory as "a doctrine worthy only of swine" (Bentham 1825: 206; Mill 1863: ch. 2).

But other hedonists take the point – and they run with it, devising variations on hedonism that accommodate the intuition that the pleasures of poetry are better than those of push-pin. Most famously, John Stuart Mill's theory "assign[s] to the pleasures of the intellect, of the feelings and imagination, and of the moral sentiments, a much higher value as pleasures than to those of mere sensation" (Mill 1863: ch. 2). Mill's view is not merely that higher pleasures have greater instrumental value – standard hedonists, like Bentham, can agree with that – but that they have greater value in themselves when magnitude of pleasure is held fixed. Two pleasures could have the same intensity and duration yet differ in value. Some think, however, that this idea is an abandonment of hedonism.

The Experience Requirement Again

There is something intuitive about the experience requirement, and this supports hedonism; but there are also interesting putative counterexamples to it. If they succeed in undermining the experience requirement, hedonism goes down with it.

The *deceived businessman* leads an enjoyable life, taking pleasure in, as he sees it, the love he gets from his family, the success of his business, and his stature in the community (Kagan 1994: 310–12). In fact, his wife is having one illicit affair after the next; his selfish children think him a fool and only pretend to love him; his business is failing on account of his partner's embezzlement scheme; and the community, who know all of this, pity rather than respect him. Suppose the businessman dies happy, never learning anything of the sad reality of his life. Hedonists will find nothing wrong with it from a self-interested perspective, but you probably didn't balk at my speaking of the "sad reality of his life." Note that the community pities him, implying that they regard his situation as an unfortunate one.

A similar, even more famous counterexample to hedonism is based on the *experience machine*, a science-fiction device that gives its users totally convincing experiences of whatever sort they would love. Suppose Nora is kidnapped in her sleep and put on the machine for the rest of her life; somehow the machine is programmed to give her exactly the same sequence of experiences she would have gotten had she lived out the rest of her life in the normal way. But now these experiences are fake. Nora won't really be summitting Everest or playing board games with her friends; it will just seem to her that she is and she will believe that she is. Did this switch harm Nora?

Many philosophers think so, but hedonism implies otherwise. Some hedonists have, in a Millian spirit, modified hedonism to deliver the result that the deceived businessman and Nora get worse lives (Feldman 2004: 109–14). For my part, I am of two minds about these cases. I can't deny that something is amiss with these lives, but it also sounds wrong to me to say that the people are actually harmed or made worse off by the deceptions. Yes, the deceived businessman was put at great *risk* of harm, since he could have discovered the truth at any moment, but, as it turned out, he skated through unharmed. What you don't know can't hurt you. So then what is amiss with these lives? Lots of things we care about are missing: respect, dignity, achievement, love, friendship. But well-being? That's less clear.

Plato's Oysterman

Plato's *Philebus* (c.360 BCE) contains a critical discussion of hedonism that imagines a life long on pleasure but completely lacking knowledge: no memory of past pleasures, no anticipation of future pleasures, no awareness of present pleasures. Socrates dismisses it as "the life, not of a man, but of an oyster." The criticism of hedonism here is indecisive (see Heathwood 2013), but the case has inspired other challenges to hedonism. Turn-of-the-century British philosopher J. M. E. McTaggart imagines an "oyster-like life" that has, at each moment, "very little consciousness," "very little excess of pleasure over pain," but lasts so long that it eventually accumulates an enormous surplus of pleasure over pain, far more than that in any actual human life (McTaggart 1927: §869; see also Crisp 2006: 630–1). Standard hedonism implies that, from the perspective of self-interest, we should all deeply envy such a life.

This isn't just a problem for hedonism; it is a challenge facing any theory that recognizes the prudential value of pleasure, even if the theory posits other, more noble goods besides. For if pleasure is good, then presumably more of it is better. Since Oysterman's life contains *so* much pleasure, that would seem to make its value swamp the value of any actual human life, even if the latter contains kinds of goods that Oysterman lacks.

One way to avoid this implication is to go in for a holistic rather than a summative approach to evaluating whole lives. That would be to say about well-being what whole-life satisfaction theories of happiness say about happiness in life. Happiness-oriented theories of well-being are well-positioned for this task.

4.2 Happiness Theories of Well-Being

Happiness theories of well-being have in common the abstract idea that the prudentially good life is the happy life. It can be made more determinate by specifying, first, what sense of "happy" is being employed in the theory, and, second, an account of this happiness phenomenon. The most straightforward happiness theory of well-being is straightforwardly equivalent to hedonism about well-being. It begins with the following set of doctrines:

The Episodic-Happiness Theory of Well-Being:

(i) Every episode of episodic happiness is basically good for the subject experiencing it; every episode of episodic unhappiness is basically bad for the subject experiencing it; nothing else is basically good or bad for anyone.

(ii) The basic prudential value of an episode of happiness or unhappiness is determined by its magnitude, which is a function of its intensity and duration.

(iii) The prudential value of a life or life-segment in itself = the sum of the basic prudential values of all of the episodes of happiness and unhappiness contained within it.

Then the view adds hedonism about happiness. To be truly complete, the view should include a theory of pleasure too. The package of views defended in Feldman 2010 does all of these things (although Feldman prefers the term "eudaimonism" about well-being over "happiness theory"). Such a theory of well-being will inherit all of the advantages and disadvantages of the hedonistic theory of well-being to which it is equivalent.

Quite a different theory of well-being, whole-life-satisfaction-based rather than pleasure-based can go by the name "happiness theory of well-being." Its distinctive claim is about the prudential value of whole lives, which it holds is determined not bottom-up, as on the episodic-happiness theory, but top-down, by the degree of satisfaction the person living the life has with their life. As before, this satisfaction can be understood as a feeling, a judgment, or some combination of the two. Sumner is the most prominent defender of this kind a view, though his view is not a pure happiness theory. For Sumner, whole-life satisfaction counts for well-being only when "authentic" – that is, informed and autonomous. We can thus understand Sumner's view as a kind of idealized subjectivist theory. One can also defend the view that life satisfaction is the sole basic prudential good without committing along the way to any views about what happiness is (as in Tiberius and Plakias 2010).

Whole-life-satisfaction-oriented theories of well-being face some of the same problems as whole-life-satisfaction theories of happiness. A person's satisfaction with one and the same life can change over time, which can yield contradictory verdicts concerning one's well-being. Animals, children, and unreflective adults who never take up attitudes toward their lives as wholes may all have worthless lives according to this theory. If a person's top-down assessment of their life very badly fits the contents of that life, the idea that the top-down assessment must take precedence seems implausible. Finally, our top-down assessments are subject to biases like duration neglect, the peak-end rule, and recency biases, and are overinfluenced by fickle moods, casting doubt on the idea that such assessments are what matters for well-being.

4.3 Desire-Based Theories of Well-Being

Finally, we arrive at the desire-based approach to well-being. I say "finally," because it is the approach I favor. This section will give an especially opinion-ated tour of its topic, including indications of where my own sympathies lie.

Desire theories of well-being hold, in a nutshell, that what's good for us is getting what we want. Although it is touched on occasionally throughout the history of western philosophy (e.g., in Plato's *Gorgias* (c. 380 BCE), St. Augustine's *De Trinitate* (416), and Thomas Aquinas's *Summa Theologiae* (c. 1274)), the theory wasn't regarded as a contender until the twentieth century, partly due to its popularity in the new discipline of economics. Probably the earliest in-depth philosophical treatment is found in Henry Sidgwick's *Methods of Ethics* (1907, I.IX.3).

Among economists, A.C. Pigou, beginning with the doctrine that "the elements of welfare are states of consciousness" but recognizing the need for something scientifically measurable, proposes that these welfare states "be brought into relation with a money measure," which requires that they be "mediated through desires and aversions" (Pigou 1920: I.5; II.1). Later welfare economists drop the underlying view that ultimate value lay wholly in the states of consciousness and come to understand desire satisfaction as not merely indicating but making for well-being. According to economist John Harsanyi, for example: "[I]n deciding what is good and what is bad for a given individual, the ultimate criterion can only be his own wants and his own preferences" (Harsanyi 1977: 645). Early advocates among philosophers include G. H. von Wright (1963), Richard Brandt (1966), and R. M. Hare (1981). "Today," some writers believe, "the desire-satisfaction theory is probably the dominant view of welfare among economists, social-scientists, and philosophers, both utilitarian and non-utilitarian" (Shaw 1999: 53).

A simple version of the view is similar in structure to hedonism:

Simple Desire Satisfactionism about Well-Being:
  (i) Every case of desire satisfaction is basically good for the desirer; every case of aversion satisfaction is basically bad for its subject; nothing else is basically good or bad for anyone.
 (ii) The basic prudential value of a satisfaction is determined by the strength of the desire or aversion involved: the stronger the desire (or aversion), the greater the benefit (or harm) if satisfied.

(iii) The prudential value for its subject of a life or life-segment in itself = the sum of the basic prudential values of all of the desire and aversion satisfactions contained within it.

Here we need to use the standard definition of "satisfaction," according to which a desire or aversion is satisfied just when its object obtains or is true, rather than the one we introduced in Section 2 for the purposes of formulating the resonance constraint and subjectivism about well-being. It follows that desire satisfactions don't require feelings of satisfaction.

4.3.1 Two Advantages and An Initial Problem

Desire satisfactionism inherits the central challenges of subjectivism, namely those concerning desires that are immoral, malicious, pointless, or base. But that is just the price of respecting both resonance constraints (the original and its cousin, the greater resonance constraint), which desire satisfactionism certainly does, and which is among its chief advantages.

Another possible advantage is that simple desire satisfactionism avoids the counterexamples to the experience requirement, which make trouble for hedonism and happiness theories. If you have the intuition that the deceived businessman would have been better off had his wife not been cheating on him, had his children loved him, and so forth – even if this had in no way affected how he experienced his life – then desire satisfactionism delivers this result. For he wants a faithful wife, loving children, and so forth, and so his actually having them rather than merely seeming to have them makes things better for him, even if he can't tell the difference between the two. Likewise for Nora on the experience machine.

Those putative counterexamples to hedonism involve pleasures based on false beliefs. Desires based on false beliefs make trouble for desire satisfactionism in a rather different way:

> Audie is out for a hike on a hot day. She runs out of water and soon becomes very thirsty. To her delight, she happens upon a remote stream. She badly wants to drink from it. Seeing no reason not to, she fills up her water bottle and drinks the whole thing down. She takes another bottleful for the walk back. But Audie is unaware that the water in the stream contains giardia parasites. They cause her to become badly ill: painful abdominal cramps, nausea, fatigue, malaise, and diarrhea, lasting several weeks.

This seems like a straightforward counterexample to desire satisfactionism. Audie got just what she wanted – to drink lots of water from that stream – but this made her worse off, not better off.

The Orthodox Solution: Idealization

The orthodox desire-satisfactionist response is to modify the theory, and in particular to "idealize" it. On a relatively simple idealized theory, the *full-information theory*, what's basically good for people is not, as on the original desire theory, to get what they actually want, but what they would want if they knew all the facts.

If Audie knew all the facts, she would know that the water contains giardia and that drinking it would make her badly ill. She thus would not, we can suppose, have wanted to drink from the stream. On the full-information theory, therefore, it was no benefit to her to drink from the stream. That is not a thing she would have wanted to do had she been fully informed.

Audie was harmed by getting what she wants. Subjects can also benefit by getting things they don't want. Suppose that Audie's upset stomach would be relieved by taking bismuth subsalicylate, a medication. Because she is unaware of this, she has no desire to take it. But, of course, taking it would still benefit her. If she were fully informed, she would know about the medication and, we can suppose, would want to take it. Taking the medication in her actual ill-informed state would thus satisfy a desire she would have were she fully informed. The full-information theory thus get this case right too.

Against Idealization

Although idealization seems promising, I believe that it is a mistake. In some cases, like that of Audie and the medication, if one is given a thing that one lacks any desire for but would want if one knew all the facts, one benefits. But not so in other cases. Your knowledge and experience pales in comparison to that of a fully informed version of you; the vast differences between you fully informed and you as you actually are creates problems for the theory. It could be that if I became fully informed, I would love eating sea urchin, reading James Joyce, and going to the opera. As I actually am, I prefer french fries, Tarantino movies, and baseball games. Moreover, if I were made to eat sea urchin, read James Joyce, or go to an opera, let's suppose that I wouldn't see what's great about these things; I'd dislike all of it through and through. It's clear that I would not be making my life better by forcing myself to do these things. But the full-information theory implies that I would benefit, because they are things I *would* want were I to become fully informed. Indeed it seems that the full-information view conflicts with the main rationale for subjective theories: things can be basically good for me on these views even if they don't resonate with me.

A popular response by friends of idealization is to move from the idealized view under discussion to a slightly more complex variation. On this "ideal-advisor view," what's good for us is to get not what our fully informed selves would want to get for themselves, but what our fully informed selves would want our actual selves to get (Railton 1986). Even if becoming fully informed would make me prefer sea urchin, Joyce, and the opera for myself, I still might, in my fully informed condition, want my actual, ill-informed self to get the french fries, the Tarantino, and the baseball that this version of myself prefers. The view would then avoid the implication that I would benefit by forcing myself as I actually am to consume sea urchin, Joyce, and opera. And perhaps Audie's ideal advisor would want her to refrain from drinking from the stream and, if she did, to treat the ensuing illness with bismuth subsalicylate.

But the ideal-advisor theory brings with it new problems. One problem is that it is at least possible that your ideal advisor finds your ignorance, inexperience, and poor taste pathetic, and, filled only with disdain for you, simply wishes you ill. My own ideal advisor might think: "If I'm ever that ignorant and uncultivated, give me sea urchin, Joyce, and opera anyway." The ideal-advisor theorist might, in response to this, attempt to modify the view by having it appeal to one's *benevolent* informed desires. She could stipulate that: "The ideal advisor's sole aim is to advance the well-being of the advisee" (Arneson 1999: 127). But such an account appears uninformatively circular. It seems essentially to be saying that what is good for a person is to get the things that someone who wants what is good for that person wants that person to get.

Thankfully, idealization was not necessary in the first place (Heathwood 2005; Lin 2019). The simple desire-satisfactionist view can deliver the right results in cases of ill-informed desires. First, consider Audie's misadventures on the hiking trail. It's true that simple desire satisfactionism implies that Audie benefits by satisfying her desire to drink from the stream. But this is actually plausible. It *is* a good thing *in itself* to quench your thirst when you are thirsty. What would not be plausible would be to claim that Audie benefits *overall*, in the long run – that, taking into account all of the effects of drinking from the stream, she is better off drinking than not. But simple desire satisfactionism does not imply this. It agrees that Audie is, all things considered, made worse off by satisfying her desire to drink from the stream. That's because if she indulges this desire, this will bring about many things to which she is averse: cramps, nausea, fatigue, malaise, and so on – for weeks. She will also miss out on lots of desire satisfactions; she'll want to spend time with friends, eat her favorite foods, and so forth, but won't be able to.

The same goes for the case of bismuth subsalicylate. Simple desire satisfactionism can accommodate the idea that it would benefit Audie to take it, even though she has no desire to take it. That's because she is strongly averse to something (being nauseous) that taking the medication would relieve.

4.3.2 Top-Down vs. Bottom-Up Revisited

A central theme in our section on happiness concerns the debate between those who think happiness in life is determined bottom-up, by aggregating episodes of momentary happiness, and those who think it is determined top-down, by how satisfied the subject is with their life. There is an analogous controversy within desire-based theories of well-being.

Simple desire satisfactionism takes the bottom-up, summative approach. *Global desire satisfactionism* takes the top-down, holistic approach. The difference here concerns clause (iii), the clause about how the value of a life or life-segment is determined (see Parfit 1984: 496–9; Heathwood 2011: 22–6).

Recall McTaggart's Oysterman, a putative counterexample to hedonism. This case makes trouble for simple desire satisfactionism too, since we can suppose that each of Oysterman's minor pleasures corresponds to a minor desire satisfaction. Because there are arbitrarily many of them, simple desire satisfactionism implies that Oysterman's life is better than the best human life there has ever been – even for those who would desire to live the latter life. That's an ironic thing for a desire-oriented theory of well-being to imply. Global desire satisfactionism avoids it. If you prefer a life along the lines of the best human life there has ever been to Oysterman's life, then, on global desire satisfactionism, it is ipso facto better for you.

In Defense of Bottom-Up Aggregation I: McTaggart's Oysterman

This is intuitively satisfying, but I think it is nevertheless wrong. I think we can show, counterintuitively, that Oysterman's life is, in fact, better. Start with a life along the lines of the best human life there has ever been. Let's suppose it lasts 100 years, and let's call it "L_{100}." Now imagine a life each of whose years is almost as good as each year in L_{100} – about 95 percent as good let's say – *but this life lasts twice as long*. This is L_{200}. Which life is better, L_{100} or L_{200}? Obviously L_{200} is. Each year in it is almost as good, and there are twice as many of them. L_{200} is in fact almost twice as good as L_{100}. Next imagine a life each of whose years is about 95 percent as good as each year in L_{200}, but it lasts twice as long as that. This is L_{400}. As before, this life is far better than L_{200}.

Perhaps you are worried that the subject will be always outliving everyone he cares about, and this will make L_{400} less desirable. But to imagine that is to imagine our thought experiment incorrectly. We are *stipulating* that each year of L_{400} is almost as good as each year of L_{200}. If the only way that that could be true for this subject is for the subject's loved ones also to get long lives, then imagine the case that way.

Perhaps you can see where we are going. There is L_{800}, twice as long as, and overall substantially better than, L_{400}. L_{1600} is far better than L_{800}, and so on. Eventually, we are going to get to a very, very long life each of whose years is only slightly good. Let's say it's $L_{1,638,400}$. It will be substantially better than its predecessor, $L_{819,200}$, which will be substantially better than its predecessor. Here's the kicker: $L_{1,638,400}$ just is Oysterman's life. Oysterman's life is thus the best life in this whole sequence. It has to be, for it is better than its predecessor, which is better than its, which is better than its, and so on, all the way back to L_{100}, the best human life there has ever been, but the least good life in the series.

Even though each step in the above reasoning looks very solid, many of us may find ourselves unable to accept this conclusion. Why should that be? It may be bias on our part. One such bias is duration neglect, which we saw in the section on happiness. McTaggart himself, who, incidentally, would accept the conclusion, also mentions our inability to properly imagine long durations of time and the fact that we tend to be enticed by large nearer term goods, which L_{100} contains, at the expense of long-term self-interest.

In Defense of Bottom-Up Aggregation II: Kraut's Baby

Recall Richard Kraut's idea that it is good for a baby to start learning a language as soon as they can, even though, being a baby, they have no desire to learn a language (Kraut 2007: 106). This looks like a counterexample to desire-based theories of well-being generally. But, in fact, it is a problem only for global desire theories.

Global desire theories will say that how good an entire possible future is for a baby, such as the future in which they start learning a language as soon as they can, is determined by how strongly the baby wants to live that future. But babies are not psychologically developed enough to have such wants. Kraut concludes that: "[T]here is no plausibility in the idea that a baby's good can be constructed out of what she wants" (Kraut 2007: 105).

If Kraut's conclusion were restricted to "what she now globally wants," this judgment would be plausible. But summative desire views like simple desire satisfactionism have no problem explaining why it is good for babies to learn a language as soon as they can. These theories determine the value of a baby's possible future by aggregating the instances of desire and aversion satisfaction within it. Babies who are taught languages will tend to get more desire satisfaction and less aversion satisfaction down the road. So Kraut's objection does not make trouble for these theories.

4.3.3 Remote Desires

Many more issues and challenges confront those attracted to desire-based theories of well-being (see Heathwood 2016), but we'll conclude our study with just one last one: the problem of remote desires. Sometimes we want things to occur that are in some way remote to us: remote in time, in place, in importance. If they come about, their coming about can seem to have nothing to do with us or our lives. But simple desire satisfactionism implies that we benefit nonetheless. The following example, due to Derek Parfit, illustrates the point:

> Suppose I meet a stranger who has what is believed to be a fatal disease. My sympathy is aroused, and I strongly want this stranger to be cured. We never meet again. Later, unknown to me, this stranger is cured. On [simple desire satisfactionism], this event is good for me, and makes my life go better. This is not plausible. (Parfit 1984: 494)

Consider also desires for things that happen after one is dead. Many find it absurd to suggest that people can be benefitted or harmed by things that happen after they are dead and gone. But simple desire satisfactionism implies that this happens all the time. Some desire satisfactionists bite the bullet here, but others agree that the problem of remote desires refutes simple desire satisfactionism and hope to remain desire theorists by modifying the simple theory.

A Restricting Solution

One popular modification restricts which desire satisfactions count toward well-being; it counts only those desires that are *about the subject's own life*. The distinction between desires that are and are not about one's own life is murky, but there are clear cases. *The stranger's being cured* is plainly an event that is not a part of Parfit's own life, while Audie's desire to quench her thirst is clearly a desire about her own life.

But this modification seems to exclude too much. Some desires that are not about oneself or one's life are nonetheless beneficial to have satisfied. When Tiger Woods won the Masters in 2019, I, a big Tiger fan, very much wanted this to happen. And it was great. Only someone in the grip of a theory would deny that this was a good thing for me in addition to being a good thing for Tiger. Note that hedonist or happiness theories of well-being would never exclude the pleasure I took in this or the happiness I derived from it. But the restriction to desires about one's own life would exclude my desire satisfaction.

Enriching Solutions

Another kind of approach aims to dissolve the remoteness by enriching the pro-attitude that plays a role in the theory. One idea is that what matters is not exactly desire satisfaction but *aim achievement* (Scanlon 1998: 118–26). Not all desires are aims. Something is an aim of someone's only if they intend to take some action to help bring it about. It is no aim of Parfit's that the stranger be cured, and so aim achievementism won't count the stranger's recovery as a benefit to Parfit.

Another idea holds that what matters for well-being is not desire satisfaction but *value realization* (Raibley 2010, Dorsey 2012, Tiberius 2018). Value-realization theories are an important recent development in the philosophy of well-being, and they are motivated by more than the problem of remote desires. (For example, consider a smoker who desires a cigarette but hates this fact about himself; because he doesn't value smoking, the value-realization theory can get the result that it is no benefit to him to indulge his desire to smoke.) We have, in fact, already looked at theories of well-being that can be classified as value-realization theories of a sort: those happiness theories that make use of whole-life satisfaction accounts of happiness that involve value-judgment-oriented notions of satisfaction. However, whereas these theories are necessarily top-down, nothing prevents value-realization views from being bottom-up, summative views.

Aim-achievement and value-realization theories are worth much consideration, but a disadvantage of each approach is that they may leave out the less lofty human goods: simple pleasures, cheap thrills (Arneson 1999: 120). If a person gets some innocent pleasure – suppose they are filled with joy for a few minutes watching two puppies playing together – we don't need to know whether this was an aim of theirs or was connected to their values to know that it made their day better. A possible solution here is simply to add pleasure or desire satisfaction to aim achievement or value realization as an independent good, although adding desire satisfaction would reintroduce the problem of remote desires. This pluralist subjectivist approach – a *subjective*-list theory – is also another possibility worth further consideration (see Lin 2016).

An Awareness Constraint

I have a different proposal for the problem of remote desires. I suggest excluding desire satisfactions when the subject lacks any awareness of the obtaining of the object of the desire.

There are two ways to go here. One way holds that for benefit to occur, three things are required: a desire for something, the occurrence of that thing, and an awareness of the occurrence of that thing. This view gets the right result regarding Parfit's stranger, of whose recovery Parfit is unaware; Tiger's victory, of which I was aware; and posthumous benefit and harm, which it disallows, since one cannot be aware of what occurs after one's death.

Subjective Desire Satisfactionism about Well-Being, Pleasure, and Happiness

That option will be most attractive to some, but there is another option, one that takes us back to the matter of the experience requirement. Standard desire theories reject that requirement, and this is usually thought of as a feature rather than a bug. It is what gets the result that many prefer concerning the deceived businessman and the experience machine. But some of us are at least ambivalent about these cases; we suspect that the deceived businessman and Nora on the experience-machine may not in fact be harmed by the ways in which they are deceived. A variation on the awareness-based solution to the problem of remote desires can get us this, if desired. This variation drops the "occurrence requirement" and holds that benefit requires just two things: a desire for something and the simultaneous belief that it occurs.

We can call states in which a way a subject wants the world to be is how they believe it to be "subjective desire satisfactions" (Davis 1981a: 116), and the theory that holds that these are the basic prudential goods *subjective desire satisfactionism*. Subjective desire satisfactionism gets the right result about Parfit's stranger, whose recovery Parfit has no beliefs about; Tiger's victory, which I do believe happened; and posthumous benefit and harm, which the theory disallows, since the dead have no beliefs. Subjective desire satisfactionism also conforms to the experience requirement, a doctrine that remains appealing to some despite its contentiousness.

Interestingly and satisfyingly, we can construct theories of both pleasure and happiness that harmonize nicely with subjective desire satisfactionism about well-being and that are plausible in their own right. Here, very briefly, is my vision.

Attitudinal pleasure just is subjective desire satisfaction: to be pleased that something is the case just is to desire it and to believe it. This attitude-based theory makes the idea that attitudinal pleasure is good conform to the resonance constraint, but it is unfriendly to hedonism in that the fundamental truth about the goodness of pleasure would be one about a certain kind of desire satisfaction.

Sensory pleasure, on this picture, is also explained in terms of desire (Heathwood 2007). It is had when one experiences a sensation that one wants to be experiencing. This account likewise makes the idea that sensory pleasure is good conform to the resonance constraint, and enables the desire approach to well-being to accommodate the obvious fact that sensory pleasures are among the good things in life.

The theory of happiness that I favor is less tidy, since I find the problem of irrelevant pleasures compelling (see Section 3.2.1). Episodic happiness occurs, in my view, whenever one gets a subjective desire satisfaction, so long as the object of the desire is not one of one's own sensations (Heathwood forthcoming). Happiness in life and dispositional happiness are explained in terms of episodic happiness in the usual way.

This is a unified, desire-oriented picture of well-being, pleasure, and happiness. It favors bottom-up aggregation over top-down assessment. It is thoroughgoingly subjectivist, or attitude-oriented. It rejects any kind of idealization. It solves the problems of remote desires and irrelevant pleasures. It conforms to the resonance constraint and the experience requirement. Is it the one true package of theories?

Reading this Element has, I hope, put you in a better position to evaluate new proposals on our topics, so I leave that for you to decide.[7]

---

[7] For a fuller defense of these ideas, see also Heathwood 2005, 2006, 2011, and 2019. Some parts of this section draw from Heathwood 2016. I am grateful to Abi Eastin, Ben Eggleston, Nicki Heathwood, Thorsten Helfer, Anthony Kelley, Eden Lin, Dale Miller, and Jason Raibley for reading full drafts of the manuscript and providing very helpful feedback, which helped me improve the Element a great deal.

References

Adams, R. M. (1999). *Finite and Infinite Goods*. Oxford: Oxford University Press. https://doi.org/10.1093/0195153715.001.0001

Annas, J. (2004). Happiness as Achievement. *Daedalus*, 133(2), 44–51. https://doi.org/10.1162/001152604323049389

Aquinas, T. (1274). *Summa Theologiae*, many editions.

Aristotle (350 BCE). *Nicomachean Ethics*, many editions.

Arneson, R. J. (1999). Human Flourishing Versus Desire Satisfaction. *Social Philosophy and Policy*, 16(1),113–42. https://doi.org/10.1017/S0265052500002272

Augustine. (416). *De Trinitate*, many editions.

Bentham, J. (1789). *An Introduction to the Principles of Morals and Legislation*. London: T. Payne.

Bentham, J. (1825). *The Rationale of Reward*. London: John and H.L. Hunt.

Bramble, B. (2013). The Distinctive Feeling Theory of Pleasure. *Philosophical Studies*, 162(2), 201–17. https://doi.org/10.1007/s11098-011-9755-9

Brandt, R. B. (1966). The Concept of Welfare. In S. Krupp, ed., *The Structure of Economic Science*. Englewood Cliffs, NJ: Prentice-Hall, pp. 257–76.

Brandt, R. B. (1967). Happiness. In P. Edwards, ed., *The Encyclopedia of Philosophy*. New York: Macmillan, pp. 413–14.

Broad, C. D. (1930). *Five Types of Ethical Theory*. London: Kegan Paul.

Buettner, D. (2017, November). These Are the World's Happiest Places. *National Geographic Magazine*. www.nationalgeographic.com/magazine/2017/11/worlds-happiest-places/

Crisp, R. (2006). Hedonism Reconsidered. *Philosophy and Phenomeno-logical Research*, 73(3), 619–45. https://doi.org/10.1111/j.1933-1592.2006.tb00551.x

David, S., Boniwell, I., & Conley Ayers, A., eds. (2013). *Oxford Handbook of Happiness*. Oxford: Oxford University Press. https://doi.org/10.1093/oxfordhb/9780199557257.001.0001

Davis, W. A. (1981a). A Theory of Happiness. *American Philosophical Quarterly*, 18(2), 111–20.

Davis, W. A. (1981b). Pleasure and Happiness. *Philosophical Studies*, 39(3), 305–17. https://doi.org/10.1007/BF00354361

Diener, E., Lucas, R. E., & Oishi, S. (2002). Subjective Well-Being. In C. R. Snyder & S. J. Lopez, eds., *Handbook of Positive Psychology*.

Oxford: Oxford University Press, pp. 63–73. https://doi.org/10.1093 /oxfordhb/9780195187243.013.0017

Dorsey, D. (2012). Subjectivism without Desire. *Philosophical Review*, 121(3), 407–42. https://doi.org/10.1215/00318108-1574436

Feldman, F. (2004). *Pleasure and the Good Life*. Oxford: Oxford University Press. https://doi.org/10.1093/019926516X.001.0001

Feldman, F. (2010). *What Is This Thing Called Happiness?* Oxford: Oxford University Press. https://doi.org/10.1093/acprof:oso/9780199571178 .001.0001

Fletcher, G. (2013). A Fresh Start for the Objective-List Theory of Well-Being. *Utilitas*, 25(02), 206–20. https://doi.org/10.1017/s0953820812000453

Fletcher, G. (2016). *The Routledge Handbook of Philosophy of Well-Being*. London: Routledge. https://doi.org/10.4324/9781315682266

Frankena, W. K. (1973). *Ethics* (2nd ed.). Englewood Cliffs, NJ: Prentice Hall, Inc.

Gay, R. (2019). *The Book of Delights*. Chapel Hill, NC: Algonquin Books.

Griffin, J. (1986). *Well-Being*. Oxford: Oxford University Press. https://doi.org /10.1093/0198248431.001.0001

Hare, R. M. (1981). *Moral Thinking*. Oxford: Oxford University Press. https:// doi.org/10.1093/0198246609.001.0001

Harsanyi, J. (1977). Morality and the Theory of Rational Behavior. *Social Research*, 44(4), 623–56.

Haybron, D. M. (2008). *The Pursuit of Unhappiness*. Oxford: Oxford University Press.

Heathwood, C. (2005). The Problem of Defective Desires. *Australasian Journal of Philosophy*, 83(4), 487–504. https://doi.org/10.1080 /00048400500338690

Heathwood, C. (2006). Desire Satisfactionism and Hedonism. *Philosophical Studies*, 128(3), 539–63. https://doi.org/10.1007/s11098-004-7817-y

Heathwood, C. (2007). The Reduction of Sensory Pleasure to Desire. *Philosophical Studies*, 133(1), 23–44. https://doi.org/10.1007/s11098-006- 9004-9

Heathwood, C. (2011). Preferentism and Self-Sacrifice. *Pacific Philosophical Quarterly*, 92(1), 18–38. https://doi.org/10.1111/j.1468-0114.2010.01384.x

Heathwood, C. (2013). Hedonism. In H. LaFollette, ed., *The International Encyclopedia of Ethics*. Hoboken, NJ: Wiley-Blackwell, pp. 2370–80. https://doi.org/10.1002/9781444367072.wbiee780

Heathwood, C. (2016). Desire-Fulfillment Theory. In G. Fletcher, ed., *The Routledge Handbook of the Philosophy of Well-Being*. London: Routledge, pp. 135–47. https://doi.org/10.4324/9781315682266

Heathwood, C. (2019). Which Desires Are Relevant to Well-Being? *Noûs*, 53 (3), 664–88. https://doi.org/10.1111/nous.12232

Heathwood, C. (forthcoming). Happiness and Desire Satisfaction. *Noûs*. https://doi.org/10.1111/nous.12347

Hurka, T. (1993). *Perfectionism*. Oxford: Oxford University Press.

Kagan, S. (1992). The Limits of Well-Being. *Social Philosophy and Policy*, 9(2), 169–89. https://doi.org/10.1017/s0265052500001461

Kagan, S. (1994). Me and My Life. *Proceedings of the Aristotelian Society*, 94, 309–24. https://doi.org/10.1093/aristotelian/94.1.309

Kahneman, D. (1999). Objective Happiness. In D. Kahneman, E. Diener, & N. Schwarz, eds., *Well-Being*. New York: Russell Sage Foundation, pp. 3–25.

Kahneman, D. (2011). *Thinking, Fast and Slow*. New York: Farrar, Straus, & Giroux.

Kant, I. (1788). *The Critique of Practical Reason* (T. K. Abbott, Trans.). Amherst, NY: Prometheus Books.

Kauppinen, A. (2013). Meaning and Happiness. *Philosophical Topics*, 41(1), 161–85. https://doi.org/10.5840/philtopics20134118

Keown, D. (1995). *Buddhism and Bioethics*. New York: St. Martin's Press.

Kitcher, P. (1999). Essence and Perfection. *Ethics*, 110(1), 59–83. https://doi.org/10.1086/233204

Kraut, R. (1994). Desire and the Human Good. *Proceedings and Addresses of the American Philosophical Association*, 68(2), 39–54. https://doi.org/10.5840/apapa201345

Kraut, R. (2007). *What is Good and Why*. Cambridge, MA: Harvard University Press.

Lamb, H. (1927). *Genghis Khan*. New York: Doubleday.

Lin, E. (2016). The Subjective List Theory of Well-Being. *Australasian Journal of Philosophy*, 94(1), 99–114. https://doi.org/10.1080/00048402.2015.1014926

Lin, E. (2019). Why Subjectivists About Welfare Needn't Idealize. *Pacific Philosophical Quarterly*, 100(1), 2–23. https://doi.org/10.1111/papq.12232

Locke, J. (1689). *An Essay Concerning Human Understanding*, many editions.

McGill, V. J. (1967). *The Idea of Happiness*. New York: Frederick A. Praeger.

McTaggart, J. M. E. (1927). *The Nature of Existence: Vol. II*. Cambridge: Cambridge University Press.

Mill, J. S. (1863). *Utilitarianism*. London: Parker, Son and Bourn.

Moore, G. E. (1903). *Principia Ethica*. Cambridge: Cambridge University Press.

Nozick, R. (1989). *The Examined Life*. New York: Simon & Schuster.

Nussbaum, M. C. (2000). *Women and Human Development*. Cambridge: Cambridge University Press.

Parfit, D. (1984). *Reasons and Persons*. Oxford: Oxford University Press.

Pigou, A. C. (1920). *The Economics of Welfare*. London: Macmillan and Co.

Pinker, S. (2018). *Enlightenment Now*. New York: Viking.

Raibley, J. R. (2010). Well-Being and the Priority of Values. *Social Theory and Practice*, 36(4), 593–620. https://doi.org/10.5840/soctheorpract201036432

Raibley, J. R. (2012). Happiness Is Not Well-Being. *Journal of Happiness Studies*, 13(6), 1105–29. https://doi.org/10.1007/s10902-011-9309-z

Railton, P. (1986). Facts and Values. *Philosophical Topics*, 14, 5–31.

Rawls, J. (1971). *A Theory of Justice*. Cambridge, MA: Belknap Press.

Rossi, M. (2018). Happiness, Pleasures, and Emotions. *Philosophical Psychology*, 31(6), 898–919. https://doi.org/10.1080/09515089 .2018.1468023

Rule, A. (2009). *The Stranger Beside Me*. New York: Pocket Books.

Scanlon, T. M. (1998). *What We Owe to Each Other*. Cambridge, MA: Belknap Press.

Schwarz, N. & Strack, F. (1999). Reports of Subjective Well-Being. In D. Kahneman, E. Diener, & N. Schwarz, eds., *Well-Being*. New York: Russell Sage Foundation, pp. 61–84.

Seligman, M. (2011). *Flourish*. London: Nicholas Brealey.

Sen, A. (1987). *On Ethics and Economics*. Oxford: Blackwell.

Shaw, W. (1999). *Contemporary Ethics*. Oxford: Wiley-Blackwell.

Shields, C. (2014). *Aristotle* (2nd ed.). London: Routledge.

Sidgwick, H. (1907). *The Methods of Ethics* (7th ed.). London: Macmillan.

Sobel, D. (2005). Pain for Objectivists. *Ethical Theory and Moral Practice*, 8(4), 437–57. https://doi.org/10.1007/s10677-005-8839-z

Sumner, L. W. (1996). *Welfare, Happiness, and Ethics*. Oxford: Clarendon Press.

Tatarkiewicz, W. (1976). *Analysis of Happiness*. Leiden: Nijhoff.

Telfer, E. (1980). *Happiness*. New York: St. Martin's Press.

Tiberius, V. (2018). *Well-Being as Value Fulfillment*. Oxford: Oxford University Press. https://doi.org/10.1093/oso/9780198809494.001.0001

Tiberius, V., & Plakias, A. (2010). Well-Being. In J. M. Doris, ed., *The Moral Psychology Handbook*. Oxford: Oxford University Press, pp. 402–32. https://doi.org/10.1093/acprof:oso/9780199582143.003.0013

von Wright, G. H. (1963). *The Varieties of Goodness*. London: Routledge & Kegan Paul Ltd.

Cambridge Elements

Ethics

Ben Eggleston

University of Kansas

Ben Eggleston is a professor of philosophy at the University of Kansas. He is the editor of John Stuart Mill, *Utilitarianism: With Related Remarks from Mill's Other Writings* (Hackett, 2017) and a co-editor of *Moral Theory and Climate Change: Ethical Perspectives on a Warming Planet* (Routledge, 2020), *The Cambridge Companion to Utilitarianism* (Cambridge, 2014), and *John Stuart Mill and the Art of Life* (Oxford, 2011). He is also the author of numerous articles and book chapters on various topics in ethics.

Dale E. Miller

Old Dominion University, Virginia

Dale E. Miller is a professor of philosophy at Old Dominion University. He is the author of *John Stuart Mill: Moral, Social and Political Thought* (Polity, 2010) and a co-editor of *Moral Theory and Climate Change: Ethical Perspectives on a Warming Planet* (Routledge, 2020), *A Companion to Mill* (Blackwell, 2017), *The Cambridge Companion to Utilitarianism* (Cambridge, 2014), *John Stuart Mill and the Art of Life* (Oxford, 2011), and *Morality, Rules, and Consequences: A Critical Reader* (Edinburgh, 2000). He is also the editor-in-chief of *Utilitas*, and the author of numerous articles and book chapters on various topics in ethics broadly construed.

About the Series

This Elements series provides an extensive overview of major figures, theories, and concepts in the field of ethics. Each entry in the series acquaints students with the main aspects of its topic while articulating the author's distinctive viewpoint in a manner that will interest researchers.

Cambridge Elements ☰

Ethics

Elements in the Series

Printed in the United States
by Baker & Taylor Publisher Services